DEDIC

When my broth........................... home in Peru we were frightened, sad and broke. The thought of living in the United States was overwhelming and by the time we landed we were already homesick.

In the pages to come you will read how we ended up on Charles and Jaxie Miller's doorstep, how I came to be a part of their family and how God used them to touch my life deeply. Little did I know that the time would come when I would sit with them in the midst of their darkest tragedies and their most beautiful celebrations, and that they would faithfully hold my hand in the middle of my own.

I gratefully dedicate this book to Charles and Jaxie and Tana and Doug and to the special memories of Kay. "When I was a stranger, you took me in."

JUNGLE CALLS

Last year the little school at Yarinacocha was officially closed after serving kids like me for fifty years. "Jungle Calls" was the name of its yearbook, and I have given the same name to this book out of appreciation to the countless teachers and staff who kept the school going all those years.

ACKNOWLEDGEMENTS

Most authors, I'm sure, write their acknowledgements after they've written everything else, thanking those who have helped. Not me. I've decided that since ackowledgements come at the beginning of the book, I should write them first as a demonstration of my faith.

Cyndi Allison will most likely do an excellent job on the cover. Her last two have gotten rave reviews and she promises me that this time my name will even be legible. Something to anticipate.

Marti Hefley will undoubtedly groan at my bad jokes, correct my jungle grammar and fuss about the fact that someone I'm referring to was never properly introduced. She will also continue to hound me for an outline but will eventually give up when the book goes to press.

My mother will provide letters and journals to jog our memories and will edit the rough copy to ensure that I don't embarrass the whole family. I will anyway.

Everyone else will tell me that I don't remember it correctly. And I will tell them that I'm sorry, but it's my book.

Table of Contents

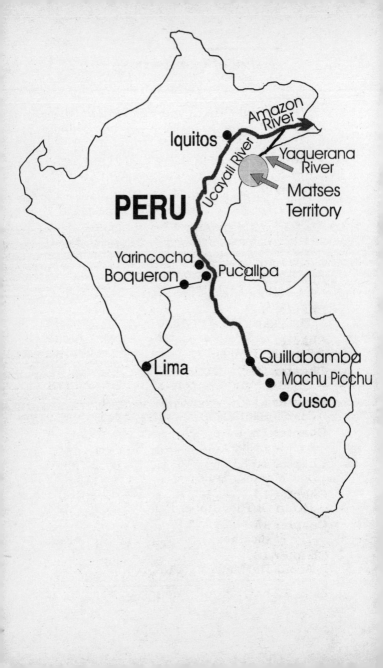

IN THE BEGINNING...

This is book III of the Rani Adventures series, and if you're lucky it will be the last. But don't count on it.

If you haven't read the first two books, you might feel a little lost when Chapter One dumps you smack into the middle of the Amazon rain forest with me. It's your own fault for not buying the whole set. If you *have* already read books I and II, you might still be lost, but then it's my fault. I'd rather blame you, so here's a synopsis. At least I think that's the right word. If not, my editor will correct it.

Shortly after I was born my parents started working with the Machiguenga Indians in the hilly rainforest of southern Peru. The Machiguengas ("Machi" for short) were an isolated, scattered group of about 7,000 who had had very little contact with the outside world. They were my first baby sitters and friends. By the time this book starts, we had known them intimately for about 18 years and the first two books cover those years.

When we weren't actually living with the Machiguengas, we lived and worked on a jungle center more in the middle of Peru. The center was on Lake Yarinacocha, from "yarina," a kind of palm tree, and "cocha," meaning lake. Although the center was very small when Dad and Mom first arrived, it had grown to a community of roughly 250 people by the time I was in high school, counting men, women and children. That doesn't include exotic pets, which easily outnumbered people at times. Apart from the Machi villages, Yarinacocha was our home.

The center personnel provided support services to linguists/Bible translators who were members of Wycliffe Bible Translators. In Peru, they worked for the Summer Institute of Linguistics (SIL) under a contract with the Ministry of Education. If you can't keep all that straight, well... neither could some of the people working there.

Just keep in mind that "SIL" refers to the organization that got us all there and kept us there, and that the Peruvian Ministry of Education wanted us to do literacy work, linguistic and anthropological research and community development projects on behalf of Peru's minority groups. From our perspective, Bible translation was a crucial part of serving the people.

Yarinacocha was a beautiful little community with aviation services, a school, a library, a maintenance and repair shop, a carpenter shop, a finance office, a clinic, a radio center for keeping in touch with remote tribal locations, a post office and administrative offices, including the field director's office. That's where Chapter One begins.

"It's time for bed," said the elderly gentleman as he lifted his wide-eyed granddaughter off my lap.

"But Pop Pop, he's telling us such funny stories," protested the giggling girl.

So Pop-Pop sat down to listen, and soon the little girl fell asleep in his arms. He laid her gently on the couch and then the two of us laughed until the tears rolled down our cheeks. And sometimes we cried. And deep into the night I told him everything I could remember about bouncing back and forth between the Amazon jungle and the concrete jungle.

When I finally went to bed, he was still sitting beside his granddaughter, one hand on her head and the other under his chin. Snoring with a smile on his face.

Chapter 1

The Volunteers

Okay, I admit it. I was eavesdropping. You'll be happy to know that at least I paid dearly for it — two weeks later I was cutting a trail through some of Peru's most isolated rainforest, and the trail could very possibly bring me into contact with Indians who had killed hundreds of men just like me. Well, most of the victims were probably older and browner than I was, considering I was just 17 and a gringo, but I still felt enough like all those other victims to not want a spear in my guts.

My only excuse for the eavesdropping is that with the walls being mostly screen in all of the houses and buildings on our jungle center in Peru, eavesdropping was a way of life. I'd grown up there, where everyone pretty much knew what everyone else was thinking and I just happened to be walking home from the post office along a path that went almost literally under the eaves of the director's office.

I only overheard a little snatch of a LOUD conversation, but it was enough to make me curious.

"...WELL, IF YOU'RE GOING TO MOVE CLOSER, YOU'RE GOING TO NEED SOMEONE TO CUT A TRAIL FOR YOU AND HELP YOU TAKE YOUR STUFF IN..."

I paused in mid step. Our field director, Rol Rich, was semi-shouting into a single sideband radio talking to Harriet Fields, who was camping in a little tent with her partner Hattie Kneeland on the banks of the Yaquerana River between Peru and Brazil. I immediately guessed that something important was going on and that the SOMEONE he was yelling about needing should be ME. Harriet and Hattie were trying to contact the ferocious Matses Indians and it seemed that after six years of patient hard work, they were getting close.

As fast as I could, I stepped into the office and volunteered to cut the trail, including as qualifications the fact that I had lived most of my life in the Peruvian rainforest. To me and my brother and sisters it was home and nothing felt so normal as high humidity, worm treatments, running barefoot through the jungle, eating monkeys, swimming with piranhas and hacking trails through the jungle. Getting speared wouldn't feel normal, but then I really didn't plan on getting speared. The optimism of youth.

At the time, SIL linguists including my dad and mom worked with Peru's Ministry of Education in over 40 different tribal groups scattered around the jungle and the Andes mountains. They analyzed their languages, described their different cultures, taught them to read and write, helped them with community development projects and translated the Bible into their languages. There were still a few jungle tribes including the Matses that had never been safely contacted.

The challenge all along had been that the Matses didn't want contact except on their own terms, which pretty much meant sneaking up on people in the dark and killing them. Actually, they didn't kill everyone — they kidnapped the women and some of the children for wives and slaves. That wasn't exactly the kind of contact that Harriet and Hattie wanted, and Harriet had worked for six years to try and figure out a healthier approach.

The Matses had valid reasons for treating outsiders that way. Rubber hunters in the early 1900s had used the Matses and other Indians for slaves and target practice, forcing them to retreat into some of the Amazon's most isolated jungle. Partly in self-defense they learned to deal quickly and severely with outsiders.

But they also needed wives. Matses men thought some baby girls were a worthless burden unless they were immediately claimed as future wives. Sort of like, "I dibs that one." If no one "dibsed," then sometimes the little girls were just strangled or left in the jungle to die. Besides that, even grown women were pretty much just tools and sometimes when the men got frustrated with them, they treated them harshly enough to kill them.

Add to that the fact that many of the men wanted more than one wife and you could see why there was always a shortage of women in the communities. For many years the Matses had made up the difference by raiding outside groups and stealing their women.

Recent attempts by the government to pacify them had included strafing from small airplanes, so now their houses were built under the jungle canopy and they quit making big gardens. Authorities in the closest city of Iquitos had records of over 1,000 killings and kidnappings attributed to the Matses, not that the Matses had actually done everything they were suspected of. Still, it was pretty clear that they were ferocious enough to have killed soldiers, lumber workers, river traders, oil explorers, neighboring Indians and anyone else who had the nerve to get close.

During her first few years of working on the Matses contact, Harriet had either worked alone or with a succession of temporary partners, taking advantage of every opportunity to prepare herself. She had studied everything she could about the Matses, had dropped gifts from JAARS airplanes into their clearings and had talked to anyone who knew anything about them. Her biggest challenge was learning the language, since it's not exactly easy to learn a language when it's never been written down and you don't know anyone who speaks it.

Her first big break came when the military base in Iquitos called to let her know that there was a woman in Iquitos who spoke Matses. The woman's name was Sophia and she had a son named Lucio. Twelve years before, Sophia's husband and children had been killed by the Matses and she was captured. The man who took her as his wife was moderately good to her by Matses standards. After all, as far as they were concerned, a woman wasn't much more than a cheap piece of property that had children and worked in the garden and carried all of the baggage whenever you went anywhere. But at least Sophia's "husband" didn't beat and torture her.

When that man was killed during a raid, Sophia was taken by another man who was just plain cruel. She began to plan an escape with her son Lucio, even though she was stranded deep in the jungle and she had seen the results of other attempts of escape. One woman she had known had run off into the jungle but was easily hunted down by the men. They cut her stomach open with a machete, forced her to carry her intestines in her arms all the way back to the village, then killed her in front of the other women.

Nevertheless, one stormy night, with thunderous rain and pitch darkness to cover her, Sophia and Lucio sneaked off to the nearest river. There they pushed a log into the swirling black current, climbed aboard and hung on for dear life as they floated away to freedom. The military heard about them and contacted Harriet.

That was the beginning. Sofia wanted to completely repress those eleven years with the Matses and get on with her life, but she did spend some time telling Harriet everything she knew about the tribe while Lucio taught Harriet some of the Matses language.

The next big break came when a patrol boat picked up a young Matses man on the bank of the Yaquerana River that marked the border between Brazil and Peru. He was naked except for a G-string around his waist when he motioned for the boat to come closer. Fearing an ambush, the captain was reluctant, but finally approached the man, whom we called "Joe."

Joe was so terrified that he didn't eat, drink or sleep during the three-day trip to Iquitos and no one was quite sure why he ever wanted to leave the Matses. He ended up in an Army hospital with a lung problem and the military notified Harriet.

Joe didn't speak any Spanish, so when he arrived at Yarinacocha to live with Harriet, nervously shifty-eyed, he depended entirely on her for everything he needed. Not that he was particularly grateful for what she did for him. He treated her, in fact, quite a lot like Matses men treat their wives, yelling at her for things she did wrong, demanding favors and ordering her around. If he was an angel sent to teach Harriet the language, he was well disguised. One historic day she finally snapped.

"You're living in *my* house, eating the

food *I* cook for you, wearing clothes that *I* provide for you, and all you do is yell and complain and order *me* around. I'm tired of it." In a nutshell, shape up! I rather imagine that was the most amazing performance Joe had ever heard in his entire life from a woman and he probably instantly regretted teaching her so much of the language. But he shaped up.

Joe was pretty tight-lipped about himself and his people, but for a year he did work with Harriet on the language when he was in the mood. We often saw Joe hunting birds with a slingshot, fishing in the lake or just staring in wonder at all the marvels on our center.

Finally Joe said that he wanted to return to his people. Harriet and a temporary partner flew with him to the Yaquerana River, where they camped together hoping that Joe would help them meet his people. He didn't, but during the weeks that they stayed there they heard a shot in the jungle, found a dead monkey on a trail and heard whistles in the dark. They were sure that the Matses were around them as they slept, but they never saw them.

"I hear the crickets singing," Joe announced one day. "I'm going to find my people." Harriet asked him to come back at the next full moon, and then he disappeared quietly into the jungle. He never returned.

Off and on during the next couple of years Harriet and her now permanent partner Hattie Kneeland camped on the banks of the Yaquerana hoping that Joe would come back, hoping that perhaps the Matses would show themselves, hoping for anything that would lead to a contact. They slept in a little tent and spent their days living and working under a small shelter that they built out of saplings and covered with a plastic tarp. They bathed in the river, talked to Yarinacocha every day by radio, studied the language and left gifts out in the jungle. Their whole world, for weeks at a time, was a tiny clearing surrounded by jungle, mosquitoes and gnats.

The next big break came from an unusual source, not that Sophia and Joe weren't unusual. A somewhat famous woman pilot, Jerri Cobb, had volunteered to do some aerial survey work for our linguists. While flying over the jungle one day she spotted a new "long house" all by itself in Matses territory. Since the Matses lived as large groups in huge houses, it was an exciting discovery and she made a note on her map and showed it to Harriet and Hattie, who immediately moved to a spot on the Yaquerana River about 20 miles from the long house. They figured that by being so close, they would certainly come in contact with the Matses. They didn't.

In the meantime, pilots and radio technicians at the center rigged up a loudspeaker on the wing of a float plane and devised ways of dropping gifts to the people that lived in the long house. Pilots picked up Harriet and Hattie, flew them over the long house and let them talk to the people below.

"Don't be afraid," they broadcasted. "We won't hurt you. Come to the big river." Down below they could see pig skins stretched on bamboo frames, drying in the sun. "Bring your pig skins and you can trade them for machetes and clothes and fishhooks. Don't be afraid. Come to the big river." Pig skins were a major source of income for many of the jungle Indians, since they hunted pigs for food anyway.

Harriet and Hattie even dangled a basket of goodies into the clearing while the pilot flew in a slow, precise circle so that the basket would hang straight down in one spot. Inside the basket was a hidden microphone so they could hear what the people were saying as they took the gifts. After all, no one knew for sure that the brown people below were actually Matses Indians. Unfortunately, either the microphone didn't work or the people didn't say anything.

The long wait continued until finally Harriet and Hattie decided to move closer.

They had been about 20 miles from the Matses long house, but halfway between them there was a small stream. They thought that maybe if they moved to that stream, the Matses would be less afraid to visit them. They started hacking a trail themselves, but it was slow tedious work. That's when I overheard the field director talking to them, and that's how I got involved.

Although I was only 17, my offer to help was immediately taken seriously. For one thing, there weren't a lot of other men who had two weeks to go cut trails through the jungle. For another, the director was reluctant to send a man with a wife and family into such a risky situation. And my dad gave me his permission, which put everyone's minds at ease. Of course, everyone who knew Dad realized that getting his permission shouldn't put their minds at ease.

Dad did have one condition that showed he wasn't just trying to get rid of me.

"Rani may have grown up in the jungle, but he's not an Indian. If he goes out there, I want him to have the best help and know-how we can get to back him up. I want a couple of Machiguengas to go with him." After nearly 18 years with the Machis Dad and Mom knew how dependable they were.

The question was, would any

Machiguengas go? The Machiguengas, my close friends ever since I was born, were a quiet and peaceful people. When they saw danger, they ran from it. Dad talked to two men who happened to be at Yarinacocha. Victorino, his neck deeply scarred from life-threatening tuberculoses as a child, had been working long hours with Dad and Mom on the Machiguenga translation work. Eduardo, handsome and bright, was at the center learning to be a small engine mechanic. They were only slightly older than I was and we had known them both since they were little boys and knew we could trust them with our lives. Even after hearing a pretty graphic description of the risks, they both agreed to go.

"We're getting the scriptures in our language and have linguists helping us," Victorino noted. "The Matses should have the same opportunity." Victorino never forgot that he was alive because of Dad and Mom's medicines.

It didn't even occur to me to be scared until we started having planning sessions. Introducing men into the contact team obviously worried people with more experience and better judgment than I had. The Matses, after all, routinely killed men, whereas they usually just kidnapped women. We spent hours discussing logistics and whether or not to take a gun and what to do with it if we did take it.

We agreed on safety precautions like always having Harriet with us, working a certain distance apart in case of attack, keeping the gun handy to shoot into the air if necessary and keeping Harriet's dog with us to sound a barking alarm in the dark. I began to wonder what it would feel like to be speared by a Matses man in the middle of the night and try as I might I couldn't make it sound like an exciting adventure.

Finally, after a week of planning and gathering supplies and equipment, we helped our pilot, Ralph Borthwick, load our food and gear into a little float plane. We kissed and hugged goodbye, belted ourselves in and headed out over two hours of endless jungle, broken only by little streams, swamps and rare tiny clearings with thatched huts in them. Even after all the time I had spent with the Machi-guengas, it was impossible to imagine what life must be like for people who never had any communication with the outside world.

On a hot Wednesday afternoon, sticky with humidity, we slalomed between the tops of overhanging trees, touched down on the narrow brown Yaquerana River and taxied to the sandy bank. Harriet and Hattie stood on the bank glistening with bug repellent and glorious tans. Their big smiles made it obvious they were eager for our help and glad for the company. Though they thought of themselves as rather average people, I got goosebumps thinking about this incredible opportunity to spend time with such extraordinary women.

As soon as we had unloaded and had some lunch, Ralph flew Harriet, Victorino and Eduardo over the long house so they could get their bearings and see what they were in for. They dropped a machete, talked over the loudspeaker and came back energized, ready to get going. Apparently the Indians below didn't look too much like killers from 500 feet in the air.

We walked a short way up the trail that Harriet and Hattie had been clearing, but by the time we'd gotten our gear organized and hung up our mosquito nets, the day had ended. We talked for a while after an early supper, filling Harriet and Hattie in on center news, then sacked out early.

As I drifted off to sleep I thought, *"So, tomorrow we start cutting our way right into the Matses heartland. What in the world am I doing here?"*

Chapter 2

The Trail Blazers

Thursday morning early. Time to get out of our beds and get our beds out of the kitchen. Time to eat some home-made granola for breakfast and go to work.

As soon as the fog lifted Ralph flew Harriet and Eduardo and me over the long house for more chattering through the giant loudspeaker under the plane's left wing as we bombed the clearing with matches and candles.

Presumably the people below, apparently shouting and waving, thought of our droppings as gifts as long as we didn't send anything through the roof of the house. They waved pigskins at us and looked excited.

When we got back to Base Camp Eddie and Vic and I each grabbed some first aid medicines, water bottles and a machete and started off up the trail. Harriet and Hattie had made a good start, but even what they had already cut wasn't quite the way we wanted it. Since this trail would be their fastest route to the airplane in case of emergencies, it needed to be wide and clear. By jungle standards, in other words, we had to make a highway. Besides, we knew we were going to have to carry all of their stuff over the trail and we didn't want branches in our faces the whole way.

It's difficult to describe what it's like cutting a trail through the rainforest, but that won't keep me from trying. For one thing, unless you've seen it, it's hard to imagine just how varied it is. In this particular area we were about 500 feet above sea level crossing very low rolling ridges. Between the ridges, in the little valleys, there were often tiny streams or wide swamps where the vegetation was impossibly thick. It could take us a couple of hours just to whack through a hundred feet of tangled vines and shrubs, and often we had to cut down small trees to make bridges across the muck.

Higher up on the ridges the undergrowth thinned out so we could actually see a hundred feet or more ahead. We were shaded by a solid canopy of tall trees high above us. If we'd been on a nature hike, it would have been gorgeous. As it was, it was difficult to enjoy the beauty when we were sweating like Finns in a sauna, constantly swatting at a million undiscovered species of flying/ crawling/jumping bugs and endlessly swinging our machetes as we hacked our way through the dense undergrowth.

There may be all the shade you ever wanted in a rainforest, but there is never the slightest whisper of a breeze down on the ground. When the sweat is running down your nose, gushing from your armpits, drenching your clothes, making the machete handle so slick you can't hold onto it and filling your shoes, you feel as if you could just get a little air, thank you very much, you could enjoy this.

Well, "enjoy" might be a little strong, but maybe "endure." There were times when the sweat spurted through the pores in our scalps so fast that if we'd been bald we'd have looked like human fountains.

Okay, so you've got the feeling now and I

won't keep saying it over and over, but I want you to keep feeling it over and over for a week. From the rising of the sun to the going down of the same, sweat and bugs and exhaustion, scratched arms and big blisters on hands and feet. Into mosquito nets long before bedtime to escape the bugs. Crotch rot because of the sweat and grime. And believe me, I *am* looking back on it from the vantage point of several years, and this *is* the funny part.

We spent most of the first day widening and tidying up Harriet and Hattie's trail and then walked back to Base Camp, almost straight into the river. I swam across it just so I could say I'd actually swum from Peru to Brazil — it took all of three minutes. Then we ate supper and discussed the fact that if we kept working from Base Camp, we'd end up doing more commuting and less cutting. It was time to move out for a night.

So, after a good night's rest, meaning only that we spent it lying down, we packed up our bedding and some food and headed out, planning to spend Friday night at the end of our trail. Harriet would go with us, as agreed in the planning meetings. Hattie would stay at Base Camp to monitor the radio and fly with Ralph over the long house periodically so she could keep up contact through the loudspeaker. Given the circumstances, it wasn't hard to imagine that the Matses thought of God as a huge female bird with a loud voice and bad pronunciation.

Sometimes Ralph would fly overhead by himself to kind of keep us pointed in the right direction. We'd yell at him through our little portable transceiver, "ET-5," when he got directly over us. Not that the portable transceiver was all that portable, since every time we used it we had to hold a fifty-foot antenna between two of us, which isn't as easy as it sounds in the jungle. It also wasn't all that reliable. One afternoon the antenna lead broke off and I had to solder it back on using a candle and a little daub of solder from another connection. It's range was so short that sometimes Ralph couldn't hear us unless he was right overhead. Anyway, as he flew over he'd say things like,

"You're right on target. About six minutes to go!"

We of course had to translate "six minutes" into days of trail chopping, with one minute of flight being pretty close to one day of chopping. It was a pretty rough measure, but it would theoretically cause us to be overjoyed with our progress. Obviously our progress in minutes could fluctuate considerably depending on whether he had a tailwind or a headwind.

At 4:00 on Friday afternoon we made

camp on a hillside, which sounds pretty early and therefore lazy except that you have to remember that it gets dark quickly in the jungle and we had to make sure we weren't eaten alive by bugs. Supper was rice and high energy meat bars that were probably military surplus from the Vietnam war. If I don't mention supper again, it's because it was always the same and I can see why it was surplus.

The best part of the evenings was when we sat beside the fire and Harriet told us stories about the Matses while we hunted for ticks and scratched bites. She was fun and full of stories and we fell asleep with fresh images of how cruel they could be sometimes.

Saturday's highlight was a monkey hunt. Since outsiders were afraid to come into the area and since the Matses didn't often hunt for anything but wives this far from their village, there was game everywhere. "Game," of course, included anacondas, jaguars and other things that would eat you before you could eat them. We saw all kinds of monkeys all hours of the day and by Saturday, just two good days into our project, we knew that our lives depended on getting something besides surplus meat bars for supper.

Vic and I did the hunting, which turned into more of a chase than a hunt. We crashed through the undergrowth with me waving our pistol in the air and him trying to get a bead with a wimpy set of bow and arrows. Our sneakers came untied as we jumped streams, crashed through bushes, landed in muck up to our calves, raced on and on stopping just long enough to see if the monkeys were still ahead of us. They always were, dropping branches and … well … droppings in our direction just to keep it all interesting. The closest thing I came to shooting was my foot when I leaped over a huge log and landed with a jolt that tripped the trigger.

You're probably happy that we never got any monkeys, but we weren't. It'd be like you eating soup and potatoes for a week and then going to the grocery store to buy meat for supper and finding out that they were sold out. By the time we got back to our trail cutting, it was time for canned tuna and crackers and candy bars, which was lunch every day.

In the middle of Saturday afternoon we headed back to Base Camp again, which was a two-hour hike by now. We plunged into the river, had supper and decided that the next time we went to work, we'd just camp in the jungle until we were either done or done in.

Sunday morning we worshipped together in both Spanish and English, swam to Brazil again, had a nice dinner and left for the end of the trail once again. We thought maybe we'd be done by Wednesday, but planned to just keep going for as long as it took. Carrying so much gear slowed us down, but the four of us still made it to a suitable campsite by 4:00.

Monday turned into our best day of work the whole week. We got up early, felt refreshed, didn't chase monkeys, hacked all morning with zest. The plane came over at noon to check our position —"5 minutes to go." A thunderstorm shook the treetops at 2:00 and drowned us but still we kept cutting, making trail and bridges like the army corp of engineers. As we progressed, Harriet shuttled our baggage along so that we wouldn't have to go back for it.

At 4:00 I went to tell Vic and Eduardo that it was time to quit. They were up ahead scouting the routing and when they heard me coming they called for me to join them. "Hmmmmm," I thought. "Something's not right here."

When I caught up with them, they were standing on a freshly cut trail and as I saw them looking it over I assumed they were trying to figure out who else might be in the area. We walked first one direction, then the other until we came to a little bridge over a creek. *I recognize that bridge,* I thought, sinking quickly into despair. A glance at Victorino and Eduardo confirmed it: we had built it in the morning. Following the sun and our noses instead of the compass that I had kept in my pocket all day, we had spent most of the day cutting in a huge circle around a high hill. Vic and Eduardo felt horrible about being such terrible route scouts. I felt terrible about never taking the compass out of my pocket.

The trail was soaked, our clothes were soaked, we were chilled to the bone, and we weren't enjoying the scenery as we made a wet camp. Harriet was graciously quiet, though she must have been wondering if this was any improvement over doing it herself.

"There's a reason why these things happen," she said confidantly, but I couldn't for the life of me think what would be a good reason for wasting the day.

We were about as miserable as I've ever been and as you know if you've read my first two books, I'd been plenty miserable before. We didn't even have a good place to bathe, since the streams were filled with leeches that lived perfectly happy lives just sort of hanging out unattached to anything until you stuck a leg into the stream and suddenly they just had to have that leg to survive. If I sound a little bitter, well, let me tell you that you're just hearing the funny part.

Tuesday, Wednesday, Thursday you can just read over what I told you before. Quaker oatmeal for breakfast, cut, hack, chop, tuna and crackers for lunch, cut, hack, chop, rice and meat bars for supper, stories to make sure we had nightmares, scratch and itch the night away.

By Friday we were so run down that we just kind of meandered along taking a swing at anything in our way as we went. Progress was pitiful and I rather imagine that Harriet was getting tired of smelling us, because she decided to go on back to Base Camp early that morning. We were to finish the trail if we could and then get on back that night ourselves. I think she didn't worry too much about us because if the Matses had attacked they'd have thought from the smell that we were already dead.

Right about then we wouldn't have cared much if the Indians had just speared us so we wouldn't have to finish the trail, but lo and behold, about the time we were ready to cash in our chips, we broke out on the little stream. Elated, we celebrated by taking a couple of hours to make a small clearing, then hauled all of our gear into the clearing and rigged a 12' x 12' sheet of blue plastic over it. We left behind the radio, clothes, bedding, and anything else that we weren't wearing.

We heard the plane come over at noon,

but Ralph couldn't find us so he flew on over to a little town on the Amazon to pick up some fuel. It didn't matter any more. He would probably have told us "three more minutes," and we would have shouted back, "check your watch, Birdman, we're here!"

It rained long and hard again while we made the clearing, so the trail was soaked. We each grabbed a handful of cookies for lunch and started back for Base Camp. We made slow progress across swollen streams and slippery hillsides and it got dark long before we reached the river. There is nothing quite like the feeling of hiking through the jungle at night, fumbling for the trail. I don't recommend it.

At 6:30 we broke out of the jungle, yelled to say that we were back and walked right into the river to wash away a full week's worth of stench. In fact, if you'll check the data you'll probably find that a record number of fish died in the Yaquerana that night. It felt so good that it's a wonder we're not still there.

In the morning we would move Harriet and Hattie to their new home.

Chapter 3

The Contact

Saturday morning it was really hard to get out of bed, even if the bed was really hard. Baggy eyes, aching muscles, empty innards after over a week of cutting trail. We were ready for a weekend of being vegetables instead of pack animals.

Still, pack animals we would be. It was time to move Harriet and Hattie and all of their stuff to their new camp smack in the middle of nothing. Then we would set up their radio, help them build a little shelter and leave them isolated and alone and patiently waiting for the Matses to come to them.

Ralph had spent the night with the airplane in a little town over on the Amazon River and hadn't been able to get back because of rain in the area. Now we waited impatiently for the heavy fog blanket to lift so Harriet could fly over the long house once more before moving. Their new camp would be so isolated that they wouldn't have access to the airplane unless they decided to walk five or six hours first.

Harriet wanted to talk to the Indians one more time. "Don't be afraid," she'd say. "We're moving closer. Come to the small river. Bring your pig skins with you."

We bundled baggage to make it easier to carry on the trail and finally heard the high whine of the plane headed our direction late in the morning. We ambled down to the sandy beach, watched it dodge the high tree branches and swish onto the river. Victorino grabbed the front of the nearest pontoon and held it while Harriet and Eduardo and I climbed in for the short flight over the long house.

"On our way there, I need you to help me find your clearing," Ralph shouted to me over the noise of the airplane after we'd lifted off. "I looked for it on the way in but I never found it." In the tall jungle, he would have had to be almost right on top of the clearing to spot it.

In a few minutes we were over the little stream and began a slow search up and down, following its tight hairpin curves. I was on the left side of the plane scanning carefully when I saw some green trees in the stream. Those would be the trees that we had felled the day before but I found it surprisingly hard to actually see the clearing even knowing it had to be there.

"It's down on your left," I shouted to Ralph. He banked left and I absent-mindedly stared at the fruit of all our hard work and wondered how a search party would ever find it again if Harriet and Hattie were in trouble. Suddenly I caught a glimpse of some movement in the clearing. Naked brown skins running out of the jungle to point and wave black pig skins. I stopped breathing, but didn't trust my eyes.

"Pineakeri matsigenga?" I asked Eduardo, knowing I could trust his eyes. His eyes, in fact, were bulging.

"Eh heh," he answered quietly. He'd seen them too, not that he'd ever show his feelings about it.

"Harriet," I shouted, "there are people down there!" My heart hammered and my stomach tightened and chills raced from my head to my heels.

Harriet came unglued and the cockpit couldn't have been wilder if we'd had two jaguars and five chickens in there. She would have jumped out of the plane if the window hadn't been so small. She leaned to the left window and started shrieking to Ralph in some unknown language that there were Indians in the clearing, but of course Ralph couldn't understand what she was saying and probably thought the engine was on fire or the wheels had fallen off. He quietly concentrated on flying the plane while Harriet and I jammed our faces into the left window and she shouted for him to turn around and I ducked out of her way so I wouldn't get squished.

When Ralph finally figured out what Harriet was talking about, he descended a little and started a slow circle around the clearing so Harriet could talk to the Indians below. There were about eight of them, all men as far as we could tell. Actually, you can tell quite a lot when they're naked, even from 500 feet up. A small canoe was tied to the bank beside the clearing.

"Come down the trail to meet us," Harriet shouted through the loudspeaker, not even knowing if these were Matses Indians. They kept waving their pig skins and Ralph kept waving our wings until Harriet had finished talking, then we flew directly back to Base Camp.

Now what?

The original plan was that if we spotted any Indians in the area, Victorino and Eduardo and I would immediately leave because of the Matses' reputation for killing men. What we hadn't planned on was seeing Indians in our clearing so soon, waving pig skins at us. In fact, if we hadn't wasted so much of Monday cutting in a circle, Victorino, Eduardo and I would have been alone in the clearing when they got there.

"There's a reason for everything," Harriet had said when we wasted the day Monday. Hmmm.

We considered various options and eventually decided to just go in and meet them that afternoon. We would at least try to find out if they were Matses and why they were there, assuming they were still there when we arrived. Victorino and I quickly volunteered to go with Harriet and Hattie, carrying some basic baggage for them. Eduardo wasn't feeling well and decided to stay with Ralph at Base Camp.

"You'll need to get your dad's permission," Harriet told me. "This wasn't part of the plan, you know." We got on the radio with Yarinacocha, told them the news and waited nervously while the radio operator there connected his radio to the telephone at our house. When Dad's voice finally boomed into the tent, I explained the situation to him and asked if I could go. I didn't have to wait long for the answer, although I can't even begin to imagine the emotions and thoughts that must have raced around in his mind.

"You've got my permission," he said. There was a brief pause. "And our blessing. We'll all be praying for you."

I wouldn't know until much later what was happening back at the center, but I'm sure you want to know *now*. I mean, *everyone* immediately asks what was going through Mom and Dad's minds, so I'll let Mom tell you in her very own words, without even editing them like she does mine. Whenever you see *this script* type, that's her story. Don't blame me if it's not funny.

It was a quiet Saturday morning at Yarinacocha. August 30 was a holiday and I was doing a bit of ironing. Probably the only reason I remember that is that when the phone call came I forgot to turn the iron off or even stand it upright so it left a permanent scorch mark on the ironing board cover.

The phone call was an extension of a radio contact with our 17-year-old son out on the banks of the Yaquerana River and the news was electrifying. From the airplane, they had seen men down in the clearing that Ron and his friends had just made. It was essential that they not "get away" before contact could be made. Time was of the essence — it would take several hours to hike in to the clearing, and it was already noon.

The question that came over the crackling airwaves was as inevitable as the answer that followed.

"Dad, I wanted to ask if I could have your permission to go in with Hattie and Harriet to help them get their gear to the clearing."

"You've got my permission," said my husband. "And our blessing," I whispered in the background. "And our blessing," Wayne repeated loudly into the phone. We knew it was possible that those could be the last words we would ever say to the tall, talented son who had already brought us so much joy in the past and who held so much promise for the future.

Within minutes someone had dialed a special code into the center's party line to signal an important general announcement. Simultaneously phones rang in every home. A quiet holiday erupted into a day of fervent prayer and barely controlled patience as we waited for the answer.

Somehow I remembered to turn off the iron as we rushed out the door to pray with our neighbors, Ted and Lillice Long. Ted was a bush pilot who had flown over the Matses long house many times to drop gifts and take supplies to Harriet and Hattie. Perhaps on those flights he had actually seen the men who were in the clearing.

Actually, the only reason I let Mom tell her side of the story is because of that part about me being tall and talented and having brought them so much joy in the past. Anyway, back at Base Camp Ralph said he would listen to the radio every hour on the hour, and we agreed that we would call him the first chance we got, assuming the radio was still where we'd left it in the clearing and it was still working. We'd had some problems with it since we spilled a bunch of honey on it a couple days before.

We started hiking a little before 3:00 knowing that we would have to push hard to make it before dark. The muddy trail slowed us down and our hard push quickly turned into a slipping, sliding scramble up and down the steep ridges. It was raining again off and on, which definitely wasn't an answer to our prayers.

At 5:30 Hattie decided that she was slowing us down too much and she wouldn't be able to make it the rest of the way that afternoon. Victorino offered to stay with her in midtrail, so we divided our meager supplies in half and Harriet and I pressed on, racing the coming darkness. We knew very well that we should never be out hiking in the jungle in the dark, but we were afraid that at first light the Indians might leave. Having seen them so close, we didn't want them to just disappear again.

At Yarinacocha, much of the afternoon passed in an interminable blur. Inevitably day turned to night as swiftly as it always does in the jungle. Someone came to fix hamburgers for our family for supper. I wasn't hungry and couldn't sit still.

Like so many of God's miracles, this one, if indeed it was going to be one, seemed to be going about things all wrong. It had never been intended that Ron would have contact with the Matses people. Much less would anyone ever dream of making contact in the dark at the end of a trail that led through swamps and over, under and around underbrush and logs and thickets that were the habitat of every kind of rainforest creature. And all in a tropical downpour! No, nobody with a speck of common sense would so flagrantly violate the cardinal rule of jungle survival: Find a campsite before dark and stay in it.

But somewhere out there in the dark and the rain and the swampy home of jaguars and anacondas, unknown to anyone but a group of faithfully praying co-workers, four people including our son trudged along with high hopes in their hearts and survival phrases on their lips. All we could do was wait.

We had five swamps to cross and didn't especially look forward to balancing on slippery sapling bridges by flashlight, especially since we'd seen signs of huge anacondas and other scary things as we'd cut the trail. By 6:30 it was pitch black. We crossed the last swamp slowly. Our whole world had been reduced to a small circle of light from Harriet's flashlight, and I kept looking over her shoulder to see where we were going.

It occurred to me more than once that something could grab me from behind and that would be that. Nevertheless I kept my own light in my pocket, conserving batteries in case we'd need them later on. Chompioshu, Harriet's dog, trotted along in front of me where I could trip over her again and again. If I'd had a spear I could have faked a Matses attack and just killed the dog. Happily.

7:15. We were worn out, but we were getting close and the adrenaline boost kept us going. I told Harriet we had just five or ten minutes to go and she started calling out into the darkness.

"We're coming. Don't kill us. Don't be afraid." Over and over again. I quietly directed her through the last 50 feet of trail toward the clearing while she shouted. The only thing I had learned to say was *"Kwasenda, Bochivo!"* or something close enough to that that I hoped it would sound like "Don't kill me, brothers!" And *"Dacurenda."* "Don't be afraid."

We entered the clearing. Nerves of steel in that woman, or at least the faith to forge ahead.

There was no one there.

The lights were on in the control tower at Yarinacocha. The static crackled endlessly. The radio *operator strained every nerve to pick up anything at all that sounded like a human voice. In homes all over the center little children were being tucked in with bedtime prayers for the safety of those out on the trail.*

I was standing by the couch in our living room when the words from Psalm 139 rushed through my mind as though they had been audibly spoken. We had read them during family devotions the day before. I hadn't memorized them, but I recalled them clearly now: The night shines as the day; the darkness and the light are both alike to you, God.

Suddenly it was all okay. All wrong, but all right. God wasn't having any trouble seeing our son in the darkness. The floodlights of heaven were shining down on the barely discernable trail, the clearing, the men who waited hidden in the jungle. Men who, we prayed, would one day experience the light of God's love themselves.

I pulled out my own flashlight and we explored the clearing. Our tarp had been moved and rigged in another spot, but there was nothing left under it. All of our gear, including the radio, was gone.

In a corner of the clearing I found a heavy bundle about 18 inches square and 7 inches thick. It was wrapped in palm leaves that had been artistically interlaced. I pried open a corner of the wrapping and saw a block of thick white paste.

"What do you think it is?" I asked

Harriet. We talked to each other quietly, like we were in a cemetery or something, listening hard for the slightest snap of a twig or rustling of a leaf.

"It's probably some of their manioc," she answered. "I think they have kind of a different way of fixing it than some of the other Indians." We speculated that it was a gift, left in exchange for our stuff.

I was starving, so I took a good pinch of the gummy stuff, popped it into my mouth and started chewing. It was sour enough to curdle my stomach and I thought that it wasn't a very fair exchange for all of our food that they got, but I kept chewing. And chewing and chewing and chewing and it wouldn't go away. We hadn't even considered the possibility of poison or drugs.

"This can't be manioc," I said finally.

"It probably is, though," said Harriet, so I chewed and chewed and chewed and finally spit it out, wondering too late if it would make me sick.

We walked over to the high river bank and shined our lights down to the water's edge. The canoe was still there, so "they" were still here. Still hiding in the dark jungle around us, watching every move we made, waiting to see what we would do.

There wasn't much we could do. We were hot, sticky, exhausted, and hungry. Our only option was to go down to the stream, wash up a bit and try to get some sleep lying on the ground. We would share the one mosquito net and blanket we had with us and hope we lived through the night, unspeared. We crawled down the bank and plunged our heads into the stream.

"Listen!" Harriet whispered urgently, water running off her chin. "I just heard something." I'd heard it too, the sound of a "yipe."

"That was probably Chompioshu," I said. "She's still up in the clearing." We finished washing and had started the difficult scramble back up the bank, Harriet again in the lead, when suddenly the jungle exploded with shouting. The Matses contact was about to begin and it didn't sound promising. Oddly enough, my whole life didn't flash in front of my eyes.

Harriet leaped the final few feet with me right on her heels. While we caught our breath we could see two lights coming out of the jungle — one a candle in the hand of a middle-aged man and one a burning stick carried by an old man. Their whole bodies trembled. They walked slowly right up to us and slapped their hands on our chests and shouted the equivalent of "Hey," "Ho," and the old man babbled, among other things, *No me mata, Papa. Tengo miedo. No me mata, Papa.* Spanish for "Don't kill me,

Father, I'm afraid."

This was no time to speculate on where he'd heard that before, or how many people had said it to him before he killed them. Harriet tried to talk to them, but they didn't hear anything she said. They shouted unnervingly, babbled on and on and loudly pantomimed some kind of wild stabbing in the jungle. *"Sahino cuero bonito, Papa,"* they'd say. "Pig skin pretty."

"Are they Matses?" I finally asked.

"I don't think so," she said.

"Oh great!" I thought. *"Now what do we do? Tell them it's been nice chatting but we've got to go and we're sorry about the mixup?"*

Mind you, things were a bit scrambled, so we have to be forgiven for missing some significant details. Harriet was trying to talk and the two men were shouting and babbling and I was getting hugged by an old man who kept saying "don't kill me" and we were wondering where the rest of the group was.

Slowly everything settled down a bit as we reached an impasse. We obviously weren't going to kill each other on the spot, but we didn't know what we *were* going to do with each other. The two men started talking more slowly and Harriet began to understand what they were saying. I saw her point to the younger man.

"That's my sweater," she said, taking hold of it's sleeve. I hadn't even noticed that he was wearing it, but what did catch my eye was the effect of Harriet's talking to him in Matses. He paused, amazed, and smiled. They were, after all, Matses! They could understand.

I looked at the older man and was startled to realize that he had on my sweatshirt. I mumbled something meaningless, motioned to the sweatshirt and pointed back at myself, vaguely wondering if pointing was a threatening gesture that would get us killed.

Instead, both men laughed with relief and started shouting again, this time toward the jungle behind the clearing. Two more young men worked their way from the darkness into the light.

They were terribly excited about having pig skins to trade. While one of the younger men went back into the jungle to get some, the middle-aged man, whom we quickly nicknamed "Clown," gave us a full blown description of how they had hunted pigs, had collected the skins like Harriet had told them over the loudspeaker, and had brought them to us.

Clown pointed to a spot in the jungle, grunted like a wild peccary, sneaked slowly over toward the site with an imaginary bow and arrow at the ready. He drew way back on the bow, let the arrow fly, then immediately jumped into the jungle to be the pig, slapping his hand over his mortally wounded heart, squealing, writhing and dying. As soon as that pig had died, he'd leap up and go after another one. We all laughed outrageously as excess adrenaline slowly burned off.

"Come with me to my house," the Clown suggested to me as Harriet translated, "and I will show you how we hunt pigs and eat them." *"Someday,"* I thought, *"I will."* In the meantime, Harriet and Hattie certainly would. Harriet had immediately refered to herself as their "Mother," as in NOT AVAILABLE FOR WIFE. Hopefully the message would be clear.

We asked them if they had our stuff, and of course they did. By pantomiming and explaining Harriet asked them to at least bring us our radio and one of the men went off with my flashlight to get it. When he came back, a little puppy came with him and it occurred to us that the puppy wouldn't have stayed in the jungle by itself. There must still be more men close by, waiting and watching. We stretched the antenna out and hoped it would still work, honey and all. It was 8:00 p.m.

"492, this is ET5," we shouted, using the airplane's identification number. No answer.

"492, this is ET5," we tried again, banging on the radio.

"ET5, this is Yarinacocha," we heard faintly from 350 miles away. Wow! They had never picked up our signal before.

"Yarina, this is ET5. We have made contact!" I shouted. "Repeat, we have made CONTACT." And then I answered a string of quick questions to reassure everyone that so far, we felt safe. We signed off to save our battery. Ralph, 10 miles away, never heard us, so Yarinacocha relayed our message to him.

It was a miracle. It was all right. Another general announcement went out to everyone on the center and spontaneously our friends and colleagues migrated to the auditorium to sing and pray. "Give of thy sons to bear the message glorious" The words of the last stanza of "O Zion Haste," were suddenly more meaningful than ever before. Then it seemed that our collective praises, carried heavenward in the worlds of "Great is thy Faithfulness," would burst right through the old metal roof and it would never be the same. Neither would we, nor the Matses.

Faithful colleagues monitored the radio frequency all night, taking turns. Others set their alarms so they could wake up in the night and participate in a prayer chain until morning. I went to bed and slept soundly the whole night through.

When Harriet asked about the rest of our stuff, the Matses men went back for candles, a clay pot full of fish and frogs, bananas and some firewood, already burning. They gave the food to us, presumably so Harriet would finish cooking it for them. I sat down on a log by the fire to roast some bananas and the old man came to sit beside me and tell me how big I was and how afraid he was. As he said it, he wrapped his arms around my shoulders and his bare legs around my waist and it seemed rather odd to be so closely hugged by a little old man who was wearing my sweatshirt and nothing else except a string around his waist.

We ate the bananas and the bony fish and stringy frogs and Clown "boinked" loudly just like the frogs, then pointed toward the jungle where we could hear the kind of frogs we were eating. In exchange we offered them crackers that didn't exactly thrill them. They nibbled around the edges and put them back into the can.

For hours we got acquainted. Clown complained of a toothache, and when Harriet explained how we fixed our teeth, he took my flashlight to examine first her mouth, then my own numerous fillings with his index finger. They felt my feet as I took my shoes off, tromped into the jungle to cut leaves for beds for Harriet and for me, dug through everything we had. The old man pulled out a tiny string hammock and strung it between a couple of saplings. They showed us how to use their bows and arrows and let me try it, this time with the real thing, and laughed wildly when they saw that I really could do it.

"What is that stuff in the green bundle," Harriet asked at one point, referring to the white paste I'd tried to eat when we first got there.

"Crude rubber," they said proudly, not knowing that the rubber hunting days were long over. No wonder it had tasted like crude rubber. If I'd wanted, I could *still* be chewing.

Since they were going through everything we had, it was inevitable that they would discover the pistol, hidden deep in my duffel bag. We didn't know if they would even realize what it was, but decided to give it to them anyway. Harriet explained that they could do with it whatever they wanted so the old man gingerly took it from me. In the morning it was sitting on a stump in the jungle, wrapped securely in vines.

Just before midnight we all lay down and I spread my mosquito net over me as a blanket. Clown joined me and snuggled close to stay warm. Clown the murderer, the child strangler, the wife beater, the new friend in my bed. I knew without a doubt that God had put it all together.

Because I was downhill from Clown, I

kept sliding off the leaves, taking the net with me. "I'm cold," he'd whimper, wrapping his arms around himself and shivering. Harriet would drag me back from semi-consciousness with her translation so I could scoot back and cover him up. We didn't sleep much. Clown and the others had a hundred questions. Were we the ones who had flown over in the airplane? Did we tell them to bring pig skins? Did we drop the gifts to them? Did we have families? Were there more of us down the trail?

Throughout the night, as questions popped into their minds they popped up to ask them, never quite accepting the fact that I couldn't understand a word of what they were saying. They'd ask me, I'd ask Harriet, and Harriet would figure it all out. I suppose they really didn't think Harriet, as a woman, was the one to deal with.

When we said there were more of us down the trail, they glanced at each other and repeated all over again, "We're afraid. Don't kill us, Father." They might have added, "Yeah, well there are more of us, too, out there in the jungle, so watch your step. *They* are."

At 3:00 in the morning suddenly everyone jumped up. A cool wind shook the treetops and brought the smell of rain. They got the plastic tarp, whipped up a sturdy new shelter and then laid back down where they had been sleeping before. During the next hour the old man got out of his hammock several times to blow loudly through his fingers. They said he was blowing the rain away and maybe it worked, since we didn't get a drop. On the other hand, I've blown loudly through my fingers several times since and it didn't do a thing.

Miraculously, we woke up at 5:45. It wasn't a miracle that we woke up that early, but that we had been asleep at all. The old man had gone, saying that he was going to get some more of his people. At 6:00 I called Ralph on the radio.

"Any chance you can fly over and circle the clearing at 7:30 or so," I asked. "We'd like them to connect us with the plane."

"Roger, roger," he answered agreeably. "Looks like we've got good weather this morning."

When they heard that the plane would be coming they whipped up some more fish, frogs and bananas for breakfast. Then they went down to the river, where they stripped off their necklaces and plunged in for baths, even vigorously sloshing their mouths clean. As soon as they dried off, someone pulled out a hairy pod full of bright red seeds and they shared it around. Each one took some of the seeds, crushed them in their hands, spit into the mush to thin it out a little and spread it on their faces, chests, arms and legs. By the time the plane buzzed overhead, they were gorgeous.

Each man wore a palm leaf headband and most had a necklace of monkey teeth. Their hair was short, apparently regularly cut with a sharp stick of bamboo or a knife. They had tattoos sort of like train tracks running from their ears down to the sides of their mouths and then in an oval around their mouths. Their upper lips were pierced about seven times so that they could put thin sticks into them, making them look like they had long whiskers. Several of them had rows of small white scars in a V shape on their chests. They made the scars by putting something from the skin of a poisonous frog on their own skin, believing it would make them better hunters. It also made them terribly sick for a few days.

They wore bracelets and ankle bands woven from palm fiber and intricately designed to adjust tightly without tying. And in between, they wore only their G-strings, which were nicely woven for special occasions or just improvised from palm leaves for everyday use.

We all waved skins at the airplane and shouted and Clown yelled at absolute top volume, "Pig skins pretty, Papa!" In the middle of the noisy confusion, with all of us concentrating on the plane, six more men followed the old man out of the jungle with fear painted all over their naked bodies. They ran up to me, threw more rolls of pig skins on the ground and quickly backed off until the plane had left. I undoubtedly looked as alien to them as a green man would to me.

While the newcomers went through all of our stuff and got a hilarious orientation from the others, Harriet asked if they would take her back to their village. The answer flipped back and forth between yes and no for quite a while before they finally decided on an answer that they could live with.

"We want to go back to our village by ourselves first," they said. "Then when the moon is full again, we'll come and get you. But first we want to come down the trail with you and see the airplane."

As we began the long hike back to Base Camp, we noticed that two of the newcomers were missing again. Although no one talked about it, we assumed they had gone back to their village to reassure everyone that they were all still alive and to report on all the wonders of the white people.

Within an hour or so we met Hattie and Victorino coming in our direction. They had spent the long, miserable wet night talking and praying to pass the time and wondering if we were still alive. At dawn they'd decided that if something had gone wrong, they were in the best position to help out. When Victorino heard Matses voices up ahead, he raced off the trail to hide behind a huge tree until he saw our white skins in one piece.

It was, over all, an incredible day with an incredible group of men. The first time we stopped to rest, we explained that we got tired faster than they did. They immediately reassured us that they were exhausted as well, and flopped down on the ground panting so we wouldn't feel badly. We all knew that they could have gone three times as fast for three times as long, but it was characteristic of them that they didn't want to show us up.

Every time we stopped they had something new to show us: how they used a special kind of leaf to sand their spears, how they had cowered behind bushes and shaken with fear when the airplane first came over their village, how their trails were made. They were quite astounded by our highway, three feet wide and nicely cleared, and graphically showed Harriet and Hattie how bad their trails were by intentionally tripping and crashing through the jungle as they ran. They gave Victorino and me each a beautiful tooth necklace made from the canine teeth of spider monkeys so they would all match in size and shape. We raced half-heartedly after some howler monkeys, showed them our medicine kit and asked them endlessly what their words were for different things.

As the day wore on, some of them went on ahead while I stayed back with Hattie. By the time we got to Base Camp, two Matses men had just gone for a ride in the airplane, flown over to their village and shouted exuberantly through the loudspeaker to their friends below. They wanted to try out the radio themselves, and sent their first message to the outside world: "We came, but were afraid. We are here, but not afraid. Everything is good."

They spent the night with us, all eight of them sleeping in Harriet and Hattie's tent, and then waited in the morning for Victorino and Eduardo and me to leave before they went back to their own village.

As we taxied away from the sandy bank in filthy clothes and monkey tooth necklaces and palm headbands, I pondered the answers to some of our questions.

What happened to Joe? His uncle killed him for contacting the white people. He had been a key figure in the whole drama, but didn't live to see it. No one ever found out why he left his people in the first place, nor why he went back. Perhaps, as we suspect, it was just that God sent him to pave the way. Joe the Baptist.

And why did the Matses finally decide to

come see Harriet and Hattie? "Because," said some of the younger men, "we were tired of living the way we were, being killed and always raiding. We decided that if you killed us, it wouldn't be any worse."

The blast of the engine reverberated throughout the jungle, Ralph pulled back on the stick and we lifted off the Yaquerana River, water spraying off the pontoons. I was on my way back to Chicago, back to college and the concrete jungle. In a few days I would be sitting in missions classes listening to professors who didn't have the slightest idea what it was like to sit on a log beside a fire in a dark clearing being hugged by someone wearing a G-string.

It was, in every imaginable way, a different world. My mind wandered back a year, when my brother and I had flown away from Peru the first time on our way to the U.S. and college. I didn't look forward to it much more this time than I had back then, and I wondered if I would ever see my Matses brothers again.

Chapter 4

Culture Shock

When Terry and I graduated from high school and left Peru, he was 17 and I was 16. With tears streaming down our family's and our cheeks, we were less ready for civilization than the Beverly Hillbillies had been for California. We had grown up barefoot and free, eating anything that walked, swam, flew or swung from branches in the jungle and thinking that dugout canoes and motorcycles and horses were the finest transportation in the world. We only had a vague sense of where we were going and didn't particularly want to be going anywhere.

We arrived in Elkhart, Indiana on a hot afternoon the second of August, 1968 and met the brave family that had volunteered to take care of us until we went to college in a few weeks. The Millers had been marginal acquaintances in Dad and Mom's home church during one of our furloughs several years before, but we really didn't remember Jaxie or the kids. Jaxie was the wife and mom and that's her real name. Her husband Charles, whom we might have remembered as our junior high Sunday school teacher, was in Australia on business when we arrived. I don't even know why they invited us to stay with them, but we weren't looking forward to it.

Jaxie invited us in and showed us to our room and we just sort of stood around gawking while she chattered away and told us where things were and her three kids gawked back at us. Maybe it was because we had immediately taken our shoes off and we had deep cracks in the calluses on our feet. Or maybe it was because our clothes were sort of antiques.

It was an incredible house. There were two whole bathrooms and I think Jaxie had had missionary guests from other countries before because she carefully explained how to tuck the shower curtain in to keep from getting the bathroom carpet wet. There was wall to wall carpet everywhere. The walls were white and clean and there was central air conditioning and color TV and the yard was nicely cut and landscaped and there weren't even chiggers in the grass. And it had an automatic dishwasher and an electric toothbrush and you could drink water right out of the taps or even the faucets in the yard and there was a basement the size of the whole house all over again.

They even had a 1968 Chevy Malibu. I think maybe they were the first people we'd ever known who had a car that was made the same year as we were living in. We were stunned and didn't quite know what to touch and what not to touch and felt totally out of place, but in spite of it all we immediately liked the Millers.

Before long we had to start unpacking, and that's when we ran into our first big problem. We opened our cardboard boxes and duffel bags and started pulling stuff out and when Jaxie walked past the door to our room she sort of hesitated and sniffed the air like a hunting dog that's caught a whiff of a pheasant. Except I don't think she thought this scent was as pleasant as a pheasant.

"Maybe you could take your stuff out in the garage until you get it sorted," she suggested diplomatically, trying not to breathe in when she talked. We piled everything back into our bags and boxes and took it to the garage and everyone kind of stood back and I think that's when Jaxie started making plans to take us shopping for clothes. She put most of our stuff in the washing machine, where it immediately lost a lot of its personality.

The kids names were Tana, 12, Kaye, 9 and Doug, 4. I think maybe "Tana" was a way for her mom to get even for "Jaxie." Doug was named for Douglas MacArthur, for reasons I don't remember. They were polite and cheerful and accepted us sort of like you'd accept the gift of a couple pet monkeys or something. We had lived in totally different worlds, but they made it as easy for us as possible to feel at home and were genuinely interested in Machiguenga robes, tooth necklaces, bows and arrows, carrying bags, monkey skulls, face paint and the like. Once they came to understand that the smell had as much to do with campfire smoke as B.O., they even got up the nerve to touch some of our things.

Our parents' home church was over-whelmingly generous and took up an immediate special offering to buy us some new clothes. I don't know if Jaxie was spreading the word or if it was pretty obvious to everyone that something had gone wrong with our wardrobe in Peru.

The first offering was $117.00 and we felt totally unworthy but I think Jaxie thought we were worthy, so armed with that exorbitant amount she loaded us into the car to start shopping. I remember thinking how strange it was that she would always save her lipstick until we were actually driving down the road and then drive with one hand and stare into the rearview mirror and hope for the best while she put it on perfectly straight. If we'd had a head-on collision, at least everyone would know right where her mouth hit the windshield.

Jaxie drove us from store to store looking for clothing that we would like and that, more importantly, would make us look like we weren't just two of her pets apes. She was a home economics teacher and a top quality seamstress and with a near teenaged girl in the house she knew everything there was to know about the current fashions. Which in those days included bell bottom pants and turtleneck shirts and leisure suits and necklaces instead of neckties. When Jaxie talked about that particular fashion, it didn't sound as if she'd be helping us shop for necklaces any time soon.

Underwear are underwear anywhere,

but when it came to buying shoes we were in deep trouble. Having spent our whole lives going barefoot, our feet were shaped like shovels with high arches, and shoes in the late sixties were shaped more like Chinese foot wraps. We marched grimly from store to store looking for something in a size 13 quadruple D that wouldn't make people laugh at us. Not that our feet were size 13 long, but they were at least that wide. It took days. Maybe weeks. And when we were done, Terry and I both had brand new shoes that we wore as little as possible.

We also needed sport coats and ties because my dad had ordered us to get some before our first Sunday in church. That took us a whole day all by itself, trying on dozens of different models and colors and textures in 10 stores in three cities until finally we ended up back where we'd started and I think Jaxie sort of gave up. I'm sure she finally just acknowledged that since our last name wasn't Miller, her reputation wasn't on the line. We thought we looked dandy, or at least thought we would if we ever wore the stuff.

In between shopping trips we had to get our teeth checked by a dentist from our church. He very generously said he'd do it for free, but I think that was before he took his first look inside our mouths. We hadn't had any decent dental care in Peru and my first appointment lasted three and a half hours while Dr. Lovan fixed 13 surfaces. I didn't know I had that many. My mouth was so numb that nothing would move anywhere and I drooled for hours.

I might have grown to really dislike Dr. Lovan's office except for two things: first, he was one of those really fun people who is interested in everything and asks lots of questions and I suppose just gets used to getting gargly answers because he has his hands in your mouth all the time. Second, he and his wife had a swimming pool in their back yard and we often got to swim there. In fact, years later he got me started SCUBA diving in that pool.

In appreciation for his kindness in pulling my wisdom teeth, I polished one of them up, flattened one side and etched the portrait of a walrus on it for a tie tack. The walrus' tusks came right down the roots of the tooth and Dr. Lovan was very appreciative. So appreciative, in fact, that for the next year he saved every gross tooth he pulled and made me a special human tooth necklace to go with my collection of monkey and pig tooth necklaces from Peru. It wasn't pretty, but I wore it anyway.

Charles arrived back from Australia in time to teach us to drive, so we could get our licenses. Of course we had taken driver's ed in high school at our little jungle center in

Peru, but we'd pretty much had to just pretend the whole time. There was only one car we could drive, and there wasn't any other traffic.

"So, *if* there was another car coming from the other direction, which side of the road would you need to be on?" Mr. James had asked. That was always a little hard to answer because there was only one lane and you'd of course want to be in the middle of it. Otherwise you'd be in the ditch. And parallel parking was a bit hard to grasp when we'd never seen any reason to do it. And we hadn't even heard about "cruising" and "dragging" and "chicken." Oh, well.

Charles wasn't impressed with our version of driver's ed, so he bravely took us out in Jaxie's new Malibu to touch up our skills. I noticed that he started off pretty much where we'd left off — way out in the country where there wasn't any other traffic. I'm sure he was pretty thorough and organized about the whole matter, since he was pretty thorough and organized about everything else, but what stands out in my mind was the lesson on burning rubber.

"You're not starting off fast enough for a teenager," he'd say. "You need to give it a lot more gas. See how fast you can get to that tree down there." After a few tries I got to where I could get to the tree fast enough to smoke the tires and please him and do credit to the Malibu. It was breathtaking. Actually, it was frightening.

"Now you've got to be able to stop a lot faster than that," he said. I think he must have been looking ahead to my driving in Chicago, rather than the more immediate need to just pass the driving test.

"See that post down there? When you get to it, hit the brakes and see how fast you can come to a complete stop." Amazing how fast it would stop if you didn't mind throwing yourself and your passengers and everything in the car against the windshield.

Although we ran stop signs and pulled into the wrong lanes and made everyone in Elkhart into better defensive drivers, we did eventually get to the place where we could pass both the written and driving portions of the exam the first time through. Of course when we proudly showed Charles and Jaxie our new licenses, he immediately starting regretting all of the stuff he'd taught us, but by then it was too late.

I give Charles and the Malibu most of the credit for the fact that I've now been driving 30 years without accident or incident. I also blame Charles for the fact that I have gotten two speeding tickets in those 30 years and can still stop fast enough to throw all of my passengers into the windshield.

My apprehension about going to Chicago

for school was increasing daily. The Democratic National Convention of 1968 filled the TV news with images of hippies and radicals protesting and rioting downtown. One night we watched as several delegates tried to pass a motion to adjourn the convention and have it at a later date. They didn't think they should try to elect a candidate for President with all of the havoc going on inside and outside the convention hall. The police had to be called onto the convention floor a couple of times and we even got to see them pick up one of the delegates and throw him out for not showing his credentials, while fellow delegates yelled "police brutality" over and over.

In Grant Park, police and National Guardsmen used billy clubs and tear gas to break up peace demonstrations, which seemed a little ironic. Rioters had blood streaming down their faces and called the police "pigs" and worse names. The city and the whole country were in an uproar and it made my primitive Indian friends of Peru seem very civilized indeed.

Terry left for college first, flying to Texas in a friend's private plane. The friend invited me to go along as well, giving us both a bird's eye view of something besides jungle. I was glad to see where Terry would be for the year, and not glad to say goodbye to him, my last link to home.

When Terry left, 4-year-old Doug moved back into his room with me. I think maybe it was an attempt to get me used to having a roommate at college. The first night went okay, but the second night he woke up three times yelling at the top of his lungs.

"MOM!" and "MOM" and "MOM" over and over endlessly, maybe replaying Douglas MacArthur hollering for his assistant. I was sure his mom would hear him and come settle him down, so I just ignored him with a pillow over my head. Where I grew up, if a kid yelled that loudly in the middle of the night everyone on the center and all the dogs would wake up!

After I couldn't take it anymore I got up and turned on the light. Doug calmed down and went back to sleep, but only for an hour.

"MOM!" I was sure they'd think I was killing him.

"What do you need?" I asked over and over. He completely ignored me.

Finally the third time, when I was beside myself, Charles came in to ask him what he wanted.

"Daddy, can you pull my covers up?" he whimpered. I could've strangled him with the covers.

The next night it was the same thing, except that it was his teddy bear he needed. And then a drink. And then... by the time I got to Moody I didn't care what kind of roommate I had as long as he slept through the night.

Charles drove me to Moody Bible Institute when my turn came. Both the sense of eager anticipation and the knot in my stomach were huge. Chicago was overwhelming with its hustle and bustle and noise and crowds of people who didn't smile or say hi or anything as they walked past.

We found our way to the campus and were dismayed to discover that it was one square block of pavement and brick buildings. Charles took me in through the famous stone arch, found the registration desk, helped me get my dorm and room number and escorted me up the elevator, our arms full of still smelly Peruvian artifacts and shiny new clothes. We found the room and went in. My roommate hadn't arrived yet, so the tiny room was dark. In the middle was a bare light bulb with a pull chain on it. I pulled, but the light didn't help much, so Charles hopefully went to the only window and pulled up the shade.

What we saw when we looked out the window was another grimy brick wall 15 feet away. Neither of us said much. Charles looked at me, remembering the stunning view I had of the lake and jungle and full moons from my bedroom in Peru. He shook my hand, said if I needed anything to let him know and sounded like he meant it. I hardly knew Charles back then, but when he left I suddenly felt all alone in a very strange new world.

Right then, neither of us had any idea how I would survive the year.

Chapter 5

Snakes in the Dorm

I lost the argument. I always do.

"Everyone will want to hear how you fared as a jungle boy in Chicago," insisted my editor.

"It's boring," I answered for the umpteenth time. "They want to read about jungles and Indians."

"You *were* an Indian," she said, probably adding an exasperated 'unnngghhh' and stamping her foot, "and you took the jungle with you. What about the snakes and the pop cans and the blow guns and the 'coon hunt in Arkansas?" The problem with my editor is that she and her family were sort of a surrogate family for me my last two years at Moody and she knows me too well.

"Okay, so that stuff wasn't boring," I gave in. "I'll do one chapter about Chicago, but if my readers hate it, I'll blame you." *"Besides,"* I thought, *"it doesn't have to be a long chapter and instead of telling it chronologically, I can just ramble through some highlights. It will throw the whole book out of order and she can just deal with it."*

The problem is I started Moody when I was still sixteen and fresh out of the jungle, so I never really felt as if I was a part of the Institute. More like an outside observer who was watching other people go to school there. That's why it always surprised me when other people felt pretty much like I was an important part of the school.

"I need you and Tim to come down to my room for a few minutes tonight," the floor monitor told me one day.

"Sure," I said, never in my wildest imagination predicting what he was going to say. He was an upper classman who took his job too seriously and walked around looking as if his relationship to God might be a bit painful.

"We've been having some problems on this floor," he said when the three of us were seated uncomfortably in his room, "and I think you two are the ring leaders." My eyebrows shot up and my jaw dropped.

"Me?" It was just my freshman year and I was shocked to be in trouble already.

"Yeah," he said, "you're always in the middle of stuff and it has gotten out of hand." I honestly couldn't imagine how he had come to that conclusion, but that's what I mean about me not feeling I was part of the school and other people thinking I was. I've never been a rebel and I tried painfully hard not to get into trouble, but I think my idea of fun just didn't fit at Moody.

I definitely didn't fit in Chicago. I had had to learn almost immediately not to smile and greet people I passed on the sidewalk, since if they were women they thought I was making a pass and if they were men, well, pretty much the same thing. It was quite a shock and seemed really sad that people would spend their whole lives stonily looking past each other.

I also could never quite figure out why it rained there. There were almost no trees to water and no grass to walk on and no rivers to send roaring over their banks. In fact it seemed as if there was almost no dirt in Chicago. Lots of grime and concrete, but no really wholesome, earthy dirt. How would anyone get really dirty in a clean sort of way?

And it was terribly noisy in a hustling, bustling, confusing sort of way. One afternoon a friend and I were walking downtown when the "El" train came over. It's a wildly noisy contraption and about the time it got directly over our heads my friend and I were crossing the street. He yelled at the top of his lungs, "RON, LOOK OUT!" and I jumped in a high spiral that landed me on the sidewalk facing the other direction. He was laughing like a madman and I wished fervently I could take him to the jungle for just five minutes. *"Dear God, I know vengeance belongs to you, but just give me five minutes alone with this guy in the jungle."*

At least we had had some serious fun on our floor in the dorm. We were quite a mixed bunch and the diversity helped. My own roommate was Ike, a very serious black preacher in his thirties. Not having had much contact with darker skins except in Peru, I automatically switched to Spanish or Machiguenga when I talked to him the first couple of weeks. He only stayed one semester and I sometimes wonder if that had anything to do with having me as a roommate. I don't think he appreciated the exuberant joy in my life when he was practicing his sermons, which went on indefinitely into the night.

Down the hall there was a Chinese

student who wanted to preach exactly like Billy Graham. He was also one of the older, more serious students. We often saw him standing with a floppy Bible draped over one hand and the other hand doing Billy Graham imitations while he practiced sounding just like the evangelist. His sing song "Engrish" was a bit of a distraction, but he had prenty of fervor and I often wonder what ever became of him. He hasn't stayed in touch with me, and I think it might have something to do with his birthday "cereblation."

We celebrated everyone's birthday by carrying them down to the common bathroom and heaving them into a cold shower. The Chinese student was rather put out by the whole thing and didn't appreciate for one moment that we were just trying to make him feel at home by treating him like we treated everyone else.

"I go by myself. I go by myself," he sing songed helplessly at the top of his lungs when we hoisted him by his arms and legs, kicking and flailing.

"You can't go by yourself," we said. "We have to carry you. It's an American tradition." I blush now to think of my cultural insensitivity, but it wouldn't be the same if he just walked down the hall and stepped into the shower. I suppose the whole thing might have been more acceptable if he'd ever seen Billy Graham being thrown into a shower, sort of like a forced baptism.

Then there was Eberline, who worked at a funeral home and always had stories about the bodies they brought in while he was on duty. Eberline was built like a linebacker and could have carried anyone he wanted to to the cold showers all by himself, but he usually let us help because it was a tribal sort of thing. Eberline's relationship to God definitely wasn't painful.

And Konrad Finck. That's his real name. He was a good friend who could make or fix anything electronic and once he even made a radio out of a razor blade and a pencil. If you want to try it, wrap a coil of wire around a toilet paper tube and run one end of it to ground and the other to the razor blade and pencil. They'll act like a diode with the pencil lead being a kind of crystal and if you attach a set of headphones just right you can listen to static all day, sort of like we did on our radios in Peru. If none of that makes any sense, it's because I got it all wrong. Except that I know he used a razor blade and a pencil.

There were a bunch of others, including the guy who had never learned to fold his own undershorts, the guy who rode a unicycle up and down the hall and then there was me. The problem with me was that I didn't speak their language. I mean, I'd grown up speaking English, but I couldn't understand these guys to save my life. The bulk of their conversations had to do with White or Red Sox and Amazing Mets and Bears and Cubs and Packers and Cowboys and people like Andy Griffith, Barbara Streisand, John Wayne and Jane Fonda. I never understood them and was always dismayed in the end to find out that sports and television and movies were far more important to them than anything else that might be happening in the world.

"Have you seen *The Godfather*?" they'd ask and I didn't have a clue whether that was a hip new way to refer to our Creator or a divine actor or some running back who worked miracles on the basketball court. Well, of course I know today that you don't have running backs on basketball courts, but back then I didn't. And not to have a favorite basketball, football or baseball team was pretty much a social sin about as bad as getting AIDS is today.

Of course they didn't understand me, either, and there were lots of times I just gave up trying to say anything about who I was.

"Where are you from?" they'd ask, and when I said "Peru" their faces would go blank and I could tell they were struggling with an appropriate response, so I'd just say "South America" before they could embarrass themselves.

It didn't seem quite fair that everyone would be more interested if I said "Elkhart, Indiana" than if I said "Peru." But if I said "Elkhart," then they'd want to know how the Pacers were doing and I didn't know if that was a new brand of recreational vehicle or a cross country running club.

Even though we couldn't really communicate, we managed to pull off a few things that took real teamwork. Like the night we figured out that the ancient elevators in our dorm could easily be manipulated from outside the elevator.

"Did you know," someone suggested meaningfully, "that if a couple of us get our hands between the doors when they try to close, they won't quite close all the way until we pull our hands out?"

"And so?" asked someone with no imagination.

"So if we leaned a stool against the inside of the doors, we could put something on the stool and send it to another floor."

That little insight opened up a whole world of possibilities and before the evening was over we had successfully leaned a thirty-gallon garbage can full of water against the inside of the elevator doors and sent it to the floor above us.

I've got to say that in general, Moody students were pretty quick to pick up on stuff like that and the guys on the floor upstairs didn't waste any time retaliating and the whole dorm would have quickly gone underwater except for one thing. We had a little genius of a guy on our floor who had studied the elevators late into the evenings when the rest of us were studying Old Testament kings. He had figured that when the elevator came to our floor, we could keep it from opening by just pressing our hands against the doors and holding them shut. Then, not knowing what else to do, it would just go to the first floor and open. Which is what it did when the guys on the fourth floor sent us back our garbage can full of soapy water.

I'm sad to say that the coach's office was right across the hall from the elevator on the first floor, and he didn't have a sense of humor. He was the same coach who taught me church history at 7:30 in the morning and gave me a D for not knowing the name and birthdate of every king and pope and reformer since God created the heavens and the earth. Anyway, he put a pretty quick stop to the elevator games and I got blamed for being in the middle of it which wasn't right because I wasn't the one who figured out the elevator.

The pop cans weren't my fault either,

even though again, I was the one who got blamed. For a long time I'd been talking about how fun it would be to make a raft out of aluminum pop cans and be the first to float across Lake Michigan on it. I had a pretty good idea of how to build it since I'd been on raft trips in Peru and I figured it wouldn't stay afloat very long but neither did Kon Tiki and that raft made some people very famous. In fact I think they wrote a best-selling book and never worked again even though their raft sank.

Anyway, the big problem was collecting enough empty cans for the raft and figuring out a place to store them. One weekend during my senior year I went to the Ozarks with James Carl Hefley, my editor's husband, who'd grown up there and wanted to show me some "real jungle." I must admit that I saw more snakes along the banks of Richland Creek where we fished than I'd ever seen in Peru and come to think of it, I'd better tell you the story of the 'coon hunt his Daddy took me on before I finish this chapter. I'll come back to it.

The point is that I got back to Moody pretty late on a Sunday night feeling really tired both from the 'coon hunt the night before and from driving with Jim, who accelerated every time a story line crossed his mind and sort of coasted back down while he chewed it over in his mind. Jim was a writer and I learned a lot from him about not writing your stories in your head while you're driving.

When I opened the door to my dorm room and flipped on the light, I couldn't see my side of the room. Not my floor, not my bed, not my desk, not my bookshelves. Everything was buried in pop cans — enough for three or four rafts.

I couldn't believe my good luck, but of course I couldn't just leave them there, either, since I had to sleep and change clothes once in a while. Over the course of a couple days I hauled all of the cans to the lounge on my floor. Moody guys were a pretty creative bunch and those cans got built into sculpture after sculpture and I thought it was probably the most entertaining thing ever to hit Moody and it was completely free.

Well, the dean of men sent me a note saying that he wanted to see me in his office and when I got there he didn't look like it was about how well I was doing academically.

"Sit down," he said, and I sat. Unlike so many of the faculty and staff at Moody, who were the salt of the earth and some of the neatest people I'd ever met, the dean of men wasn't terribly friendly or understanding.

"I want those pop cans out of there in two hours," he began and ended.

"What am I supposed to do with them?" I asked, wondering if I was going to be thrown out of school. "I mean, it wasn't me who brought them all in."

"I don't know and I don't care. Two hours." I still have a hard time understanding why someone with the Creator of Joy and Laughter and Love and LIFE in his heart could be so grouchy.

Well, I only had a couple of choices: I could throw all the cans out my window on the ninth floor or I could dump them all down the laundry chute. I'd better not say which one I did, because no matter what I did, someone out there will think I made the wrong decision.

The blowguns were just a case of primitive technology that got out of hand. I never should have introduced them to my dorm, but then I didn't realize how troublesome they'd be in the wrong hands.

It took a long time to develop a blowgun for Moody. The ones I'd seen and used as a child in the jungle were made by Indian craftsmen who took two pieces of wood over eight feet long and sanded a groove in between them using a slender stick and some sand. The best grooves weren't quite straight, but curved a bit to compensate for the sag in the long blowgun. When the groove was just right they rounded the outsides of the two pieces and wound a flat piece of thin bark around them. It was a very complicated process and no one I knew at Moody was clever enough to do it, so we had to come up with something different.

You, of course, might think that we didn't have to come up with anything at all, since people had functioned quite well in Chicago for almost 150 years without blowguns. This isn't the place to get into a discussion like that — just accept the fact that it seemed important to me to have a blowgun.

In the end I discovered that electrical conduit is perfect, since it's a relatively lightweight kind of pipe with no bumps or seams on the inside. We took 12-inch sections of metal clothes hangar wires for darts and wrapped one end with masking tape and sharpened the other end. Then we took turns practicing on various targets. When we got more skillful we practiced on laundry carts in the basement, since we could get them moving pretty fast down the halls while we shot at them. Hitting moving targets is essential if you're going to hunt rats in the inner city, which was our final goal. We even made a few students dance once we got better, which was especially fun because dancing was forbidden at Moody.

I'm sure most of you can't imagine how there could be anything wrong with all of this. We were having good clean fun and helping clean up the city at the same time and you're probably about to go make your own kids some blowguns. Well, I have to warn you that blowguns give some people a sense of power that's hard to stop. Ours delivered such an impact that the darts would go three quarters of an inch into the walls of our dorm, and unfortunately, when we tried to pull them back out little chunks of the walls would come with them. That's when I learned how to patch sheet rock, and that's why the dean of men outlawed blowguns at Moody. Mind you, I've made quite a lot of money patching sheet rock since then and it was probably one of the most practical things I learned there.

The snake thing was just an attempt to add some life to our rather sterile dorm. All I did was ask my parents to bring me a couple of boas from Peru when they came for a short furlough one summer. They tucked them into little handbags and carried them on the plane and right through customs. Nowadays that's against the law, but back then I think customs officials didn't feel it was that important to be putting their hands into bags with snakes in them, so they just waved them through.

I thought snakes would be perfect pets for a dorm room because they don't make noise, don't have any odor, don't eat much and just sort of lie around all the time. I mean, have you ever seen a boa constrictor fetching a ball or jumping on the furniture or chasing the mailman?

My snakes were about four feet long when I met them, and growing fast. I named them Sophoclese and Periclese, but could never really remember which was which and it didn't matter anyway since they never came when I called them. They were beautiful and became an instant sensation on my floor and guys came in pretty often to experience the indescribable sensation of having a boa squeeze them around the arm or neck. There's just nothing quite like it and if the snake is big enough it can be a once in a lifetime experience.

Well, before long other guys were buying snakes at pet shops and getting some pretty big ones. Unfortunately they weren't all as careful as I was with the snakes and soon there were horror stories floating around about janitors who'd pull the cover off an air conditioning unit and come face to face with a six foot boa. No one got bitten or squeezed or swallowed, but a few tottery old maintenance men had heart attacks.

Boas only need to eat every few weeks or so, which is nice, but they only eat live things, which isn't so nice. We had to do some creative thinking when it came time to feed them, and not everyone appreciated our solutions. The most efficient meals we came up with involved buying white mice in bulk from a laboratory supply house. We would blockade one of our rooms, throw all fifty mice and all eleven snakes into the room and then invite everyone in our dorm to watch. Sort of like the Roman amphitheaters, I suppose.

It was an awesome spectacle that pitted nature against nature in the same old primordial struggle that's ended up with mice inside of snakes ever since creation. The snakes actually looked pretty lethargic, just slowly slithering on their bellies with their tongues doing most of the work until they starting homing in on a mouse. Then they'd gradually curl their bodies up into coils and curves like they were getting ready to fall sleep or something. When they were pretty sure they were in striking distance all of a sudden there'd be a blur. We'd all jump and so would the mouse, but it would usually be too late and before we or the mouse could blink it would be all wrapped up.

It was awesome to watch each snake swallow four or five mice and I suppose we did get a little carried away with the excitement of it sometimes. Like when we started naming the mice, using names of less popular deans and faculty members, and then betting on who'd go first. Not betting money, of course, but just sort of keeping track.

The dean of men hated the snakes. That would be the same dean of men who hated the pop cans and the blowguns. Before long he called a meeting of the snake owners and we all gathered in what was becoming a pretty familiar place to me.

"The snakes have got to go," he said with about the only smile I ever saw. "I asked Dr. X." I do remember Dr. X's name, but I'm not including it because what he said would probably embarrass him when he looks back on it and I know that the majority of the Bible scholars at Moody would have disagreed with him.

"In the Garden of Eden," he began, "the serpent tempted Eve and when Adam and Eve sinned, God cursed the serpent. Knowing that, we don't feel that it's appropriate to have snakes in the dorm."

"Good grief," I thought, *"next they'll be telling us we can't eat apples at Moody!"*

Well, there's no arguing with theology like that, so the snakes disappeared one by one. I, of course, had nowhere to take my snakes and wasn't about to put them in the Chicago sewers, so I prevailed on the Hefley family to host them temporarily. Jim didn't care for them much, but Marti didn't particularly mind getting up in the middle of the night to restrain them when they started knocking things off the shelves in the bathroom. Once a mother always a mother. Eventually I passed them on to a friend whose parents didn't know that snakes had been cursed.

Which brings me back to the 'coon hunt in Arkansas and then we're done with my days in "civilization."

James Carl was mighty pleased to be back in his ol' stompin' grounds in the Ozarks for a weekend with his ma and pa. He reckoned we could go fishin' and hikin' and eatin' squirrel's brains and 'coons and other vittles and his ma and pa reckoned they'd pack us fuller 'n a hog gut in a sausage factory.

Don't worry if you don't know what all that means — I couldn't understand them either. The bottom line is that everyone thought it would be a great idea for me to go raccoon hunting one night because I'd hunted so much in Peru. We piled into a rattly old pickup truck with a couple of 'coon dogs and headed into the woods and I sort of wondered how we'd ever keep up with the dogs in the dark.

Well, hunting coons isn't like hunting anything else I've ever hunted. Grandpa stopped in the middle of some place that must have looked like 'coon country and let the dogs out of the truck and then we just sat there in the truck talking and listening to the dogs and trying to stay awake. It was about as exciting as visiting in an old folks home.

After a half hour or so Grandpa suddenly sat up straighter 'n a bean pole.

"They got one," he said.

"They did?" I asked with barely controlled enthusiasm.

"Yep. Yuh cain tell by the way they're barkin'." Of course I couldn't tell anything by the way they were barkin'. I was just sort of wondering why nobody put g's on the ends of anythin'.

We turned on our flashlights and headed off through the woods toward the dogs and after crashin' through the brush five minutes or so we could see them makin' a racket at the foot of a whoppin' big tree. The 'coon had apparently clumb the tree and was hidin' in a hole about twenty feet offn' the groun'. They don' use many d's on the ends of words either.

"James Carl says you growed up in the jungle," said Grandpa in a way that made my blood run cold. "Clamb thet tree and scare the 'coon out."

Well, you may think from reading my books that I only have half a brain, but the half I had was working really fast. I instantly remembered times in the Machiguenga villages when hunting dogs would corner animals sort of like 'coons and the dogs would come back all cut to ribbons, their skins just hanging off them in bloody strips. I couldn't think of anything less appealing than clambing that tree in the dark and scaring a 'coon out of his hole, but my reputation was on the line and they were waiting for me. So I clumb.

I even clumb pretty fast cuz I was full to the scalp with adrenaline and even Grandpa had to reckon I was a pretty good clumber. I clumb right up to the 'coon's hole and broke off a branch and kind of poked it around in thar with one hand while I hung onto the branch with the other and hoped like crazy the 'coon would just stay put and we could all go home and clumb into bed. But suddenly he busted out of there in a terrible rage and I thought my life was over and I only vaguely remember Grandpa and James Carl laughing lak they had roaches in their armpits or sumpthin'.

The 'coon couldn't see too well because of the lights on him and he hit the ground with all four legs burning rubber, but the dogs were ready for him and they got into a tussle like I'd never seen before until Grandpa finally grabbed the 'coon by the tail and picked him up and backed the dogs off and made a space so I could skid down the tree and catch my breath and slow my pulse back down.

Grandpa handed me a burlap bag and told me to hold it open so he could put the 'coon in it and I thought the opening was a little small considering how far the 'coon could reach and how mad he was but since my reputation was at stake I did it anyway and that's how we ended up back at the house with a live 'coon in a burlap bag and I've never even tried to tell my Machiguenga friends that story because they would think I made it all up. Yes, I know those sentences are a little too long, but you have to remember that I was kind of hyper at the time.

Well, that about sums up Moody and if I tell you any more you'll just get bored. In between the fun and games there were a lot of stretches of just trying to survive the frigid winters and the homesickness, but there were also lots of friends who kept me going. Charles and Jaxie Miller often drove clear to Chicago to pick me up for holidays, and I spent many a relaxing weekend with Jim and Marti Hefley and their three girls and their dog, Frisky.

I suppose I'd better add that most of my struggles with Moody were because I was a confused foreigner even though I didn't look like one. The school itself was a fabulous educational experience and I'm very grateful to the faculty and staff that worked sacrifically hard so that I could get a top quality understanding of what I believed and why.

I even learned some valuable things while I was there. I learned that there's way more to the Bible than anyone will ever master, and that there are some extremely bright people who love God deeply and that Christians come in all sizes and shapes and quirks and that you can study a lot about God without ever getting to know Him and that if you're going to have friends you have to take the first step even when you feel really odd. And I learned that there are some pretty needy people right in the U.S. and that where you are isn't as important as who you are, although I can't say I learned that too well because most of the time I wished I was back in Peru.

I also learned that God takes care of His children in little ways, like the day I was so broke I couldn't afford to mail my parents a letter and then found a stamp on the ground on my way to class. And in big ways, too. Like the time I walked into the registrar's office to tell him I had to drop out for lack of funds and he said he had just gotten off the phone with an anonymous friend who called to say he'd like to pay my tuition for the semester.

I was one of the two senior class speakers at graduation and I still don't know quite how it happened. Ironically, I'm writing this chapter as I take my second son to his first year of college. After an orientation meeting this morning a woman suddenly called out to me from across the room, "Did you go to Moody?"

"Yes," I said with a big question mark on my face.

"I thought so," she said. "Ron Snell. I was in your class. Twenty-seven years and you haven't changed a bit." I'm still amazed that anyone would remember I was ever there.

But once again I've gotten way ahead of myself. At the end of my freshman year I went back to Peru for the summer, and it's high time I took you back there with me.

Chapter 6

The Raft Trip

When Terry and I exited the Faucett jet on Pucallpa's burning hot runway in June of '69 and felt the humidity of the Peruvian jungle instantly wilt our clothes, we knew we were home. Our first year at college in the U.S immediately faded into the distant past and the delicious smells and sounds of the dusty rainforest flooded in. For three months we were free.

There were a number of

missionary kids who came home to Yarinacocha that summer along with a flood of guest helpers. The guest helpers were high school or college kids who came from all over to work on special projects and learn a little about life as a Bible translator. They were always fun to have around with their wide eyes and neurotic fears of anything that creeped or crawled.

One group of eight high school students came from a Presbyterian church in South Carolina. Four guys and four girls and a 24-year-old sponsor named Alleene — all with hilarious accents, though they didn't think so. They worked hard and played hard and everyone on the center fell in love with them. Since the children's home was empty during summer vacation, the South Carolina gang stayed there with Uncle Jim and Aunt Anita, who were normally the house parents. Those of us who were "natives" of Yarinacocha took it on ourselves to make sure they had a memorably good time.

Like the night I threw a five and a half foot iguana into the girls' room. I had a good excuse, of course — they had swiped my motorcycle key and wouldn't give it back.

"If my key doesn't come flying out of there by the count of five," I said, "this iguana is going to come flying in." I wouldn't ordinarily have had the nerve, but Aunt

Anita had told me that they were expecting something awful and I shouldn't let them down. Aunt Anita is like that.

"You wouldn't dare," they answered without much confidence. "We're not decent."

"It's a female," I countered, "and it won't care." I jerked open the door, bent down and flung the iguana across the floor as far as I could into the room. It came alive in an instant and hit the floor scrambling with all of its sharp claws, scattering girls as it went. Their screams could literally be heard halfway across the base as they leaped to the top bunks and cried hysterically for me to come in and get the iguana. Funny thing, they didn't sound southern when they screamed.

"You're not decent," I said matter-of-factly, "and I haven't seen my motorcycle key yet." Up in the living room, Uncle Jim and Aunt Anita were laughing so hard there were tears in their eyes.

Well, I got the key back and I'm sorry to say Alleene had to go before the Center Discipline Committee because her kids were making so much noise so late at night and someone had complained. That's the trouble with screen walls.

Unfortunately Alleene didn't trust me much after that. The next day we all went by plane to visit a Machiguenga village and

Alleene wouldn't speak to me except to say, "We're not talking about it." She was pretty upset and didn't even care when I reminded her that the iguana was probably more upset than she was. Anyway, that's what I mean by helping them have a memorably good time.

Somewhere along the way I thought it would be a memorably good time for the guys and me to go on a raft trip. We could make our own rafts out of something, launch them somewhere and float on them to somewhere. There were a few minor details that I didn't figure out until later.

The guys were enthusiastic about it because they hadn't a clue what they were getting themselves in for. Alleene wasn't at all sure her kids should spend that much time with me, but she eventually gave in and, to her credit, became a great supporter.

On a brutally hot, muggy Saturday five of us took a speedboat down the lake to a low lying area where there was a grove of balsa trees big enough for rafts. The trees were about a mile from the lake and in between there was a kind of miserable swamp filled with lily pads and colonies of floating ants and vermin of all kinds that would eat you without a second thought. The only way to get across it was to paddle a couple of tiny dugout canoes. Chuck and Bobby went first and managed to make it without swamping. Unfortunately Chuck slipped and fell in trying to get out of the canoe. Bruce and David both turned over. I made it without dumping, but the canoe was so full of water I got soaked anyway. It was an ominous beginning.

It took all day to hack our way through the jungle, cut down twelve trees with machetes and axes and strip the bark and branches off them. Without the bark they were a good bit lighter, but also covered with a mucous kind of stuff that made them as slippery as ... well ... snot. Like a peeled grape.

Somehow no one, mostly meaning me, had brought any drinking water so we nearly died of heat exhaustion and dehydration. By the time we started carrying the logs back out to the lake, staggering through the jungle and tripping over roots and vines, everyone was ready to mutiny and the rafts weren't even built yet. The good news was that we'd all gotten over our fear of dying, so we ignored the canoes and just swam through the swamp alongside the logs. By then, nobody cared what might eat us on the way across.

During the long miserable day everyone got acquainted with isula ants, since each balsa tree had its own nest of them. Isulas are giant mutant ants about an inch and a quarter long and when you disturb their nests they make a frightening racket, squinching and squeeking and rattling their sabers by the dozen. One good sting from an isula and you'd be in bed for the better part of a day with headache and other aches and it would be memorable but not a good time.

Anyway we dehydrated ourselves and scraped the skin off our hands and shoulders cutting and carrying and when the day was over we only had half of the 12 logs we needed. We towed them back to the center, hauled them up to my house and left them to dry out until we could get the rest two weeks later.

After five weeks we had three beautiful rafts four feet wide by ten feet long and had finally decided what route we would float. They looked perfect sitting in my back yard lashed together with pegs and crossbars and rope, but I did have to wonder if they'd be big enough to float two guys each for three or four days. There was no shortage of people coming by to give us their opinions and advice.

Some people were really excited about the whole project and wanted to go along. Others thought it would take twice as long as we planned. Quite a few thought it was a ridiculous idea and we'd sink as soon as we climbed aboard. I felt like Noah and hoped Alleene was listening to the

optimists. The good news was that Bruce
Kindberg, who'd grown up alongside me in
Peru, had agreed to come along so we'd have
an even number on the rafts.

We collected a bunch of mismatched gear
including reed mats for sunshades, two air
mattresses, blankets, a little kerosene stove
and boxes of food that weighed almost as
much as the rafts. That was because
Alleene, in a gesture of forgiveness and
generosity, offered to buy all our food for the
expedition. Her boys might never come
back, but at least they would die full of
brownies, pudding, cookies and other
essential nutrients.

The air mattresses were a sort of last
resort against the rafts being too small — if
the balsa sank, we could get to shore on the
mattresses, we thought. Besides, since the
rafts would be hard to paddle and steer, we
could use the mattresses sort of like
dinghies.

I shopped around for a truck to take us
sixty miles to the launch site on the
Pachitea River and couldn't find anything
affordable. Uncle Jim rescued our trip by
offering to take us in his pickup truck free
of charge if we'd haul 1,000 bricks to the
children's home for him. We hauled!

We loaded Uncle Jim's pickup on a
Friday night. It sagged badly under the
weight of the three rafts so we decided Bill

and I would follow along behind on a little Honda 90 motorcycle. We all sacked out in the children's home, but didn't sleep much what with the growing excitement and a big robbery going on at my house and Chuck getting sick. Don't worry, you'll get to read about the robbery later.

We left at 4:30 in the morning, hoping to launch as the sun came up. The pickup kicked up so much dust that Bill and I dropped way back and bounced along in a thick fog. The dirt road was in fairly good condition so we were making pretty good time with Bill driving, when suddenly a rough bridge popped into view with its first planks about 5 inches higher than the road. Bill hit the brakes too late and we dropped into a chuck hole, then slammed into the front edge of the bridge.

As we bounced into the air I saw him going over the handlebars and didn't have time to think of much except *"grab Bill and the edge of the bridge!"* I did, so that when we landed I had one arm around Bill and the other arm around a plank on the bridge and we were hanging halfway off, thirty feet above a little stream. The cycle was on top of us.

"Are you okay?" I asked Bill. He nodded uncertainly. "Well then, you're going to have to move first, because I'm hanging over the edge." He got up and limped off the bridge, popping a dislocated finger back into its socket along the way.

I'd gotten a bit of a scrape and Bill had a sore knee, but the cycle didn't fare quite so well. The front forks were bent, the brake lever twisted back, one light knocked out and the shift lever bent. We climbed back on anyway.

Wouldn't you know another bridge popped into view fifteen minutes later and I couldn't stop any faster than Bill had, especially with the bent brake lever.

"Hang on," I shouted over my shoulder, and instantly got a bear hug. We slammed into the first plank and bounced high in the air, landing six inches from the left edge of the bridge. I jerked the handlebars to the right on impact and we bounced again when we hit the edge of a rough plank. Landed in the middle of the bridge, hit the brakes and climbed off until I stopped shaking.

Still the hardy cycle kept running, so we climbed back on and took off again in pursuit of our companions. When the third bridge came into view, Bill leaped off the back and let me go by myself. See? He did have a brain.

By the time we got to the river's edge the others had only been there ten minutes. They'd gotten slowed down by a cow they hit, but both the truck and the cow were fine, they said. We unloaded the rafts and launched them without even a christening, which was probably bad luck. Then we piled our baggage on and shoved off into a stiff current.

Since I designed the rafts myself, I'd like to say that they were perfect, but I'd be lying. They had a few flaws that soon became clearly apparent. Like the fact that four feet by ten feet looks pretty big in a pickup truck but not nearly so big on the river. And the fact that the sun shade arrangements weren't particularly sturdy. And the even worse fact that one of the rafts was a little too far underwater when Chuck and Bobby got on board. Bruce and David immediately discovered that a colony of fire ants had a nest in one of their balsa logs and the ants weren't happy about being submerged. Still, there would be no turning back. Uncle Jim had already left, cutting off our retreat.

The sun was ferocious. Our little shades barely kept the sun off us and the wind kept blowing them over. In the days before sunscreen, that was catastrophic and we soon looked like six boiled shrimp rafting down the river. We spent the whole first day making sure that we'd get skin cancer in later life, constantly adjusting the sun shades and learning how to control the rafts so we could avoid things that looked as if we should avoid them. Every time we went ashore clouds of gnats attacked and drove us underwater for refuge, so we didn't stop much.

The current was never fast enough to give us a thrill, but it moved along and even gave us a bit of a riffle here and there, just wavy enough to get our gear wet, which was pretty easy considering we were almost underwater anyway. When we got too hot we jumped overboard to swim with the alligators and sting rays and orifice fish. If you don't know what orifice fish are, ask your mommy. We kind of caught up on sleep and walked along the banks hunting unsuccessfully and ate a lot. Chuck still felt a little sick and all in all I'm pretty sure it was more memorable than fun.

Unfortunately, as soon as the sun went down the mosquitoes realized that a six-course pre-cooked dinner had come to town, and the mosquito nets we had didn't want to stay up any better than the sun shades. So now we looked like six dancing boiled shrimp rafting in the dark.

It sort of goes without saying that none of us had ever been on this particular river before, so I had no real idea how long it would take us to get to Pucallpa, the nearest river port to Yarinacocha. I knew the river wasn't particularly dangerous in terms of rapids unless we hit a log or something, but no one I knew had ever rafted down it. To hedge our bets and to stay as far from mosquitoes as possible, we decided to post a watch and just float through the night. I'm not saying it was a good decision, just that that's what we decided.

"If we're going to float all night I think we'd better tie the rafts together," I suggested as the sun went down.

"Won't that be a problem if we hit something?" asked someone whose brain hadn't yet been completely fried.

"Yeah, but it'd be worse to wake up in the morning and not know where each other was," I answered. It was a silly answer, of course, because it assumed that any of us would actually sleep. We tied the rafts together so we could keep track of each other in the darkness. We had a great view of the Milky Way — it was our own way we couldn't see very well, even though the moon was nearly full.

We set up our wet bedding and put away the supper stuff and Chuck dried the dishes "I guess I'll just have to forget my cultural past," he said as he carefully wiped forks and spoons and knives with a pair of underwear, which was the only dry cloth he could find.

There wasn't much to do but look at stars and listen to each other complain about wet blankets and narrow beds. Bobby and Chuck grumped the most, both insisting that they didn't want to sleep hanging in the water even though their blanket had fallen in and I couldn't see how it was all that different.

"Let's go alligator hunting," suggested Bobby, who loved hunting anything anywhere anytime. Gator hunting was a pretty common pastime in those days, in part because the meat in the tail is delicious.

"With what?" several of the guys asked at once.

"We'll go on the air mattress and take the .22," I suggested, making it sound like the most obvious thing in the world. By then there was only one air mattress because Chuck had jumped onto the other one during the day and exploded it.

In the end only three of us decided to go, which was probably good because the air mattress was really made for just one. Since we didn't want to get our clothes wet before going to bed, we just completely stripped and climbed aboard, all three of us sort of hanging off the edges.

Looking back on it, of course, I'm really embarrassed. Not that we were skinny dipping, but that we were dumb enough to go alligator hunting naked on an air mattress in the dark. I mean, what in the world did we think we'd do with a 'gator if we got one? And what if one got us?

We shined a flashlight along the shore watching for bright red eyes reflecting in the light, and when we saw some we'd quietly paddle up as close as we could. I'd have to say that was one good thing about the air mattress — it was quiet. Then we'd take aim right between the eyes and squeeze off a shot, but I'm sorry to say we didn't get any. It's a little hard to hold the rifle steady with three guys on an air mattress, especially since the closer we got to the 'gators the more we wriggled and scrambled trying to get as much of ourselves as possible on the mattress.

We actually did get one small one by just reaching out and grabbing it, but it hardly counted and we let it go so it wouldn't scratch or bite holes in our skin or our mattress, or attract its mother with its loud grunching. After two hours we finally gave up and went to bed.

The next morning we had a pretty good hunt just walking along the banks of the river, but got a ways behind the rafts. Three of us ended up running along the bank, leaping fallen trees, tearing through knee-deep mud, jumping off cliffs and finally just plunging into the river when the jungle got too thick along the shore. Bruce and David were on the air mattress and Chuck, who still wasn't feeling all that well ended up alone, asleep on the rafts. He suddenly woke up in the middle of the river far ahead of us and wondering if we'd all been killed by alligators or kidnapped by pirates. He tried shouting for us, but we were too far behind him. Frantic, he tried to paddle the rafts around some bushes in the river but couldn't, so he just tied up to them which was the only reason we ever caught up.

The rest of the day we fished without catching anything, hunted without shooting anything, baked in the sun, swam and watched the muddy banks go by. The only real break in the routine came when we paddled the air mattress to a village to shop for bananas and the villagers were having a big celebration and we turned out to be the best part of their show. We hand paddled back with our stalk of bananas feeling like we had contributed to their joy.

"Let's spear some sting rays," I offered to relieve the oncoming boredom. Not that sting ray hunting is all that exciting, but at least there's a bit of a chance of getting hurt, so it keeps you alert.

Two of us swam to shore and sharpened a couple of long poles. Then we walked along the shoreline looking for pock marks in the muddy bottom, where sting rays were likely to be waiting for someone like us to step on them. By walking carefully, looking sharp and jabbing hard, we eventually got three of them and whacked off their vicious tails.

As fun as the alligator hunting had been the night before on the air mattress, we all knew that there was no future in it, so during the day we paddled over to a little village and bought a dugout canoe. We were delighted to pay so little for it and the seller was probably elated that we paid so much for it, considering how rotten it was and how badly it leaked. Still, it struck us as a colossal improvement over the air mattress and well worth the twenty dollars.

The Pachitea emptied into the Ucayali River early in the afternoon, reducing our speed and the prospect of danger to about zero, we thought. The Ucayali is wider and muddier, being one of the two main tributaries to the Amazon farther down. Its millions of gallons of water flowed along at a steady 5-6 miles an hour, headed for the Atlantic Ocean. We caught up on sleep and had just survived the worst heat of the day when I heard the drone of a small airplane.

Having grown up in villages where the infrequent drone of an airplane meant mail and goodies and news from the outside world, Bruce's and my ears immediately perked up and we scanned the sky for a tiny moving speck. In those days it almost had to be an airplane from Yarinacocha heading out to a village.

We saw it at the same time, flying

surprisingly low over the river, quickly growing from a black spot into a Helio Courier with floats.

"Hey, everybody wave things at it," I shouted. We picked up whatever bright and colorful things we could and waved them over our heads in a form of low tech greeting.

The plane came right overhead and then banked and turned and started to descend.

"Oh no!" Bruce moaned. "Stop waving. He thinks we're in trouble. It costs a fortune to land those planes and take off again and we'll have to pay for it. Shoo him away."

We tried to shoo and look safe and comfortable, which isn't all that easy when you're sinking. Anyway, there was no stopping him now. He touched down with a splash and taxied right up to our rafts. Then he shut off the engine, climbed out and threw us a rope. I was dismayed.

The passenger door opened. I blinked and looked twice, not trusting my eyes. Out climbed Aunt Anita, a cooler full of ice cream in her arms and a big smile on her face. Behind her came Alleene, Georgia, Shannon, Ellen and Jo Ann. Uncle Jim had chartered the flight so everyone could see how we were doing and bring us some frozen salvation. I suppose he knew better than most that the rafts might all have sunk by now.

Alleene was visibly reassured at the miracle of seeing her kids still alive in spite of having just spent two days and a night with me. We didn't immediately go into the part about hunting alligators naked on the air mattress.

They tried climbing on the rafts with us, but only stayed for a few minutes since they couldn't get on the rafts without completely submerging them. We all chorused thank yous and they flew off into the sunset, leaving us to the mosquitoes.

It was a splendid evening. The sun set in a blaze of oranges and reds. On the other horizon the full moon rose, spilling a trail of silver down the river. Even the freshwater dolphins were inspired — a couple dozen of them put on a show for us, racing in circles around our rafts and leaping high out of the water in unison, just for fun.

Our alligator hunting took a great leap forward that night, what with the canoe and all. There wasn't a lot of freeboard, but at least we were all completely out of the water. I would aim the canoe at a pair of bright red eyes, Bobby would shoot at it when we were seven or eight feet away and Bill would grab it as we sped past. At least that was the theory. In practice it was harder than it sounds, but finally we got one about six and a half feet long. We hefted him into the canoe, put him in the back where I was sitting and kept hunting.

"This thing sounds like it's still breathing," I whispered to the other guys. I couldn't see the gator, but kept hearing something like long sighs and groans, and since it's head was between my knees in the bottom of the dugout I was getting a bit nervous. Once I even thought I glimpsed some movement, but that had to be impossible, since we'd shot it right in the head.

The rest of the night was fruitless. Although the current was relatively slow, it turned out to be a little difficult to spot the gators, maneuver between fallen trees and logs, hold even with the flow and shoot all at once in the dark in a canoe that tipped easily and leaked constantly. We eventually gave up and went to bed.

In the middle of the night I suddenly bolted upright to the sound of a loud splash right beside the rafts.

"What was that?" Bill wondered in long Southern syllables. It amazed me that they even spoke that way when they were half asleep.

"Must've been a big fish," I assured them, looking around to reassure myself.

In the morning, our gator was gone.

I could bore you with the details of the third day, but just because we had to endure it doesn't mean you have to. Another day, another night, another three and a half million mosquitoes. We were all thinking that a two-day trip with a hotel in the middle would have been about right.

Just before the sun rose on the fourth day we saw signs that we were getting close to Pucallpa. The river traffic picked up considerably, the trash along the shores became obnoxious and in the distance there were plumes of smoke from plywood factories. We started preparing for our arrival back in civilization, putting on a few more clothes. In a sacrificial tribute to our crummy canoe we dumped a bunch of gasoline in the bottom of it and threw in a match. It made a spectacular 25-foot torch as it drifted off, and heralded the dawn.

About the time we could actually see Pucallpa, we could also see a big tree stuck in the river up ahead. Our rafts were still tied together and pretty hard to maneuver, so well ahead of time we started arguing about which way to go around the tree. Chuck said left and I said right and by the time we had decided to go right, the current was swinging left and going a lot faster than we had realized.

"Hang on," I ordered. "We're going to hit it." So, paddling frantically, we smashed broadside into the tree, with Bill's and my raft leading the way. It tipped up against the tree trunk, so that Chuck and Bobby's raft on the other side buckled right underneath the other two, spinning us all around and taking Chuck and Bobby with it. All I could think as we watched for them to surface was that they were probably pinned between the rafts or hung up on tree branches and how could this happen within sight of Pucallpa? This certainly wouldn't do anything for my relationship to Alleene.

Bobby popped up first, then Chuck with a big gasp. I inhaled a big breath to match Chuck's and we immediately plunged into the river to recover as much of the drifting baggage as we could. Then we paddled furiously so we wouldn't just drift right on past Pucallpa. We unloaded what was left, waded ashore in septic mud up to our armpits and called my parents for a ride home, where we put the rafts in the lake so the little kids on the center could use them for Huck Finn adventures.

Alleene thanked me for giving her boys such a fun, safe trip and I said … "Uhhhhh … you're welcome."

Chapter 7

The Robbery

In the last chapter I mentioned a robbery that kept us awake the night before our raft trip. Who ever would have thought that our little dog Chico would play such an important part in it?

To be perfectly honest, Chico wasn't much to brag about. In fact, to be even more perfectly honest, he was a pain in the neck, yapping endlessly about anything that crossed his mind. None of us would

ever have expected that we'd be so grateful
to him, but to tell his story, first I have to
tell you a bit more about Yarinacocha and
our house.

Yarinacocha was a beautiful place to live
and work. As you would expect in the humid
jungle, lots of things grew there, including
buttercup flowers and orchids and grass
and hibiscus and mildew and termites.
Visitors often commented on how it was a
tropical paradise, but of course they didn't
have to mow it. I don't think anything you
have to mow qualifies as paradise.

Things even grew where you didn't want
them to, so that if you slept too long during
rainy season, you'd wake up to find your
leather shoes were green or a vine had come
through the window. Or you'd suddenly find
a patch of fungus growing on you in a place
where you couldn't even show your friends
how gross it looked.

Our houses didn't have air conditioning,
so they were built with walls and doors
made primarily of screens. If we were lucky,
a breeze would waft clear through the
house. That's how we always knew what
our neighbors were having for dinner, or
that it was time for them to change their
kid's diaper. If we were unlucky, a violent
thunderstorm would blast halfway through
the house, flapping the curtains like flags
and washing everything in its path.

The roofs started out thatched, but somewhere along the line the thatch was replaced with corrugated metal, which sounded much nicer in a rain storm but was so hot in the middle of the day that you could blister your bare feet on it. Fortunately most roofs eventually got a bunch of mildewy crud on them, which insulated them a bit. They all had their share of leaks, so we all had our share of pans and bowls and cans to put under the leaks. That was a pretty good source of drinking water back in the days before the addition of a centralized water treatment plant.

It's got nothing to do with this story, but I might as well add that every house had some way of collecting rain water because back in the early years the only piped water came straight from the lake and had ... well ... things swimming in it. Our house had a nice rectangular cement cistern about four feet long and three feet wide sitting on high posts right under the gutters in back. If we were really lucky, the cistern would have water in it all through the year. Otherwise we'd have to boil lake water.

Of course I'm still a little confused as to why we so confidently drank water out of that cistern when we wouldn't think of drinking lake water. I can remember having to climb up to the water tank and clean it out every once in a while. Usually it was because it started smelling like dead rats, and usually that was because there were dead rats in it. But along with the dead rats we often scraped out whole armloads of algae, moss, frogs, lizards and other things that have never been scientifically classified. Even a dead possum once, whose leg just sort of came off when we tried to lift it out of our water supply.

The foundation of our house was pier and beam, which means that a sort of low concrete wall went around the perimeter of it and then a bunch of brick piers held the floor up. There was one hole in the perimeter so a contortionist with nerves of steel could crawl under and inspect the bottom of the house.

Foundation inspections were a pretty regular part of our life cycle because the termites thought the brick piers were put there just for them. They'd make long tunnels out of spit and dust and then scavenge the house for books and sentimentally precious photos to eat. They were so good at it that they could eat the guts right out of a whole row of books and leave the covers looking as good as new.

Anyway, my brother Terry and I usually had to do the inspections, armed with a little can of arsenic powder and a spoon. Mind you, once we got under the house there was only that one little escape hole and we knew all about boa constrictors and

bushmasters and scorpions and brown
recluse spiders and guerilla terrorists and
a thousand other things that might be
hiding down there. It didn't matter that
some of those things had never been spotted
in the Amazon jungle — the whole point
was that they might be discovered for the
first time right under our house. We hated
those inspections, slithering around on our
backs while our sisters bounced around in
the house shaking dust into our eyes and
ears and noses.

Nowadays, of course, if our parents told
us to go dump arsenic into termite tunnels
and our eyes and ears we could call Child
Protective Services and that would be the
end of it. Instead we lived and breathed
arsenic all those years and who's to say
what we might have become without all
that stuff in our brains. Like I might be able
to tell a story without getting so distracted.

I think that's why missionaries often
hesitate when you ask them how many children
they have. They're trying to decide if they
should tell you how many they've ever had, or
just how many are still living. It wouldn't
surprise me to find that I have more brothers
mummified under the house at Yarinacocha,
for example, covered in arsenic. I know I've seen
pictures of little boys in our family that don't
look anything like me or Terry.

Well, the good news is that most of the

house was made out of mahogany and the termites didn't like it. They don't have expensive tastes. So even if they did eat our libraries and albums, they at least left the shelves alone.

The point of all this, in case you've missed it, is that we had screen walls and doors, which aren't very secure. Dad even refused to lock the doors because he said if the doors were locked then thieves would just slit the screens, and he didn't want to have to be fixing screens all the time. All of the houses at Yarinacocha were built the same way, so you could say security was minimal.

Although Yarinacocha began its life as a relatively isolated little center in the middle of nothing, it wasn't long before other communities grew up around the lake. They weren't exactly on top of us, but they were close enough and we were very fortunate that the vast majority of the people were completely trustworthy. In fact, many of them worked on our center. The occasional thief could wander in and swipe something, but usually it was pretty small stuff like mangoes or a few clothes off the line in the back yard. If you could have seen how we dressed, you'd wonder why anyone would want to swipe our clothes.

Unfortunately, as transportation between our center and the nearest city got better, more people began to see potential in our screens. That led to increased thievery and a lot of discussions about what we should or could do to improve the security. Some of our members were in favor of putting a barbed wire fence completely around our center. Some even thought it would be appropriate to put a high brick wall around it, as almost any Peruvian organization in our shoes would have done, but the majority of the members argued vehemently that we were guests in Peru and were there to serve the people rather than lock them out.

It was a discussion that went on and on for years and was made even more difficult by the fact that we all knew we had much more than our Peruvian neighbors. Ironic as it seems, it felt a bit unfair to make it harder for people to steal our stuff. Some of us probably even felt like it was a good way to get rid of some of the hand-me-downs we had to wear.

There were even a few great stories to come out of the thievery, which made it easier to tolerate. "Uncle" Scotty, who lived just down the hill from us, heard from a tattle-tale that someone in a village down the lake was selling stolen goods. He went to check it out and saw a mattress for sale. Since it looked familiar, he stopped and turned it over. Sure enough, in big black magic marker letters it announced on the bottom: "This mattress was stolen from

Gene Scott." We were on furlough in the U.S. that year and didn't know that our house had been gutted by thieves. Uncle Scotty retrieved most of our stuff from the same yard sale and when we got back from furlough it was all back in place without our ever knowing what had happened.

Well, high principles aside, it didn't seem very smart to just let people carry off ALL of our clothes and appliances and motorcycles. During the summer of '69, organized thievery had become a serious problem, to the extent that a neighborhood watch was instituted and all of the center's dogs were on full alert.

Chico was one of the center's dogs, but being on alert mostly meant listening for the sound of the cookie can opening. Sad to say, most of his descendents, of whom there was a vast number, were no better than he was at learning anything useful. In fact, when I said that all of the center's dogs were on full alert, that wasn't intended to mean that they would do any of us any good in an emergency.

Chico's distinguishing feature was his tail, which was wound into a tight circle that looked a lot like a teacup handle. His children and grandchildren all had the same tail, and I often thought that if we could somehow freeze those tails, we could just hang them all up in a meat locker when they were being particularly annoying.

Some people would have never let them out of the locker.

Mind you, the Chico style dogs weren't all that bad when you consider that the other huge majority of the dogs on the center were weenie dogs, of which there were so many that someone suggested changing the name of the place to Purinacocha. Can you imagine trusting all of your earthly possessions to the watchful eye of a dog that can't even turn a tight corner without backing up? Weenie dogs are interesting to look at, and some even had a primitive form of brain, but I've never seen one on a police force.

The most interesting of the weenie dogs were the psychotic fetchers. They'd fetch absolutely anything that anyone threw, including lemons, rocks, balls and firecrackers. I probably shouldn't admit it in public, but that opened up lots of fun possibilities, including the common practice of showing a weenie dog a brick and then throwing the brick into about four feet of water.

Anyway, as part of the center's security force, Chico wasn't very promising. He was only about a foot tall at the shoulder and often had a quizzical look on his face indicating he didn't know what was going on, which was probably pretty much the case ever since his car accident when he was a puppy. The only thing he had going for him as a watchdog was that he never smiled. I mean, some people, including the weenie dog owners, said that their dogs could smile, but we never even had to pretend that ours could. He was just a grump.

He was also lucky. Lucky, for one, to have us as owners, since we are a very tolerant family. Lucky also to be alive, in more ways than one. In my last book I told how he got hit by a car and Dad actually paid to have him treated. I can't help but think that the only reason Dad would have spent that much money on a dog noisier than himself was that he was hoping Chico would get a little bigger before we ate him.

Chico went for a ride once with Dad and a Peace Corp volunteer, and managed to jump out of the Jeep while no one was looking. He hadn't quite thought through the length of his leash in relation to the length of the jump, so he ended up hanging himself. That would have the been the end of his short life if the Peace Corp volunteer hadn't given him mouth to mouth resuscitation. The Peace Corp guy didn't realize until too late that the only way to bring peace to Peru was to let Chico die.

In Monte Carmelo, a village where the Machiguengas had real dogs for hunting, Chico was mistaken for something besides a dog and a big black monster picked him up, crunched him to the bone and shook him, hundreds of miles from the nearest vet. He eventually healed, of course, but the experience had to have done something to what was left of his brain.

He was even stolen once by an Indian in a canoe. It took a couple days to get Chico back, which kind of surprised us because we all thought the Indian would have gone berserk within 15 minutes trying to shut him up.

Anyway, Chico was lucky to be alive and still a part of our family, even if he wasn't an essential part of the center's security force.

And now, finally, my story is coming together: houses with minimal security, a growing population around us that included a few organized thieves who had repeatedly robbed houses on the center and a dog that had long since lost everyone's respect.

It was late at night. Terry and I were gone for the night, everyone else was asleep and the doors weren't locked. A dark form padded up to the side door, quietly turned the knob and slipped into the house. Tiptoed past the kitchen, past the living room and study where Chico slept at full alert. Tiptoed, for some unknown reason, past my parents' bedroom and into the bathroom, where he took a used toothbrush, dirty clothes and an electric razor without the cord. The brashness of it all is still pretty amazing, but probably the dark form had been in our house before.

Anyway, Chico finally woke up and starting growling. That isn't particularly interesting, since he always immediately started making noise when he woke up. What was amazing was that the growling woke Dad and that Dad actually took it seriously, pulled on some shorts, walked into the hall, nearly bumped into the dark form and startled both of them. The dark form immediately headed for his escape, Chico now barking furiously and Dad right behind him.

I'd like to report that Chico the hero dog leaped high in the air and grabbed the thief by the throat, but no, Dad had to do that part. Dad lunged at him from behind and the guy took off running out the same door he'd come in and down the red brick sidewalk through our back yard. He whipped hard left at the road and raced hopefully toward the edge of the center with Dad right behind him in high volume pursuit. If you read my first book, you know that Dad has a voice that could call ancestors back from their graves, so when he hollered the whole center and the neighboring village woke up. Unfortunately he wasn't thinking too clearly and was yelling in Machiguenga, which no one including the thief could understand.

The thief's escape route took him past the Borthwicks' house, just down the hill from us, where Wayne and Vern were spending a summer home from college in Canada. Wayne and Vern were big guys and even half asleep they could move pretty fast. So now the lone thief had quite a posse of grim white faces in his wake and it's a safe bet that he thought his life was about over.

To make a short story of a long chase, Dad caught up first and remembered enough of his teenage wrestling skills to get a hammer lock on the thief. The thief didn't know much about the finer points of wrestling — he just twisted around enough to get a good bite on a couple of Dad's fingers and it was pretty much of a stalemate with Dad upping the pressure on the guy's neck and the guy crunching Dad's fingers with a pressure that Chico would have envied. Chico's teeth never quite lined up after the car accident and I think it added to his attitude.

"You'd better ease up or you'll break his neck," a newly arrived grim white face suggested to Dad.

"I'll ease up when he quits biting my fingers," said Dad

Uncle Herb was kind of on security at night, which was lucky because he was in charge of the cattle program during the day and when he hog-tied something it stayed hog-tied for a long time. He was the one who tied up cows so they would make the long flights out to various villages without kicking out the sides of the airplane.

When he got done with the dark form, it stayed hog-tied on the ground until someone decided to lock him up in the finance office while they waited for the police to come. I'm still a little mystified as to why you'd lock a thief up inside the finance office, but maybe no one was thinking too clearly in the middle of the night. On the other hand, maybe it was because it was the only building on the center with a lockable door.

Well, under Peruvian law in those days, thieves weren't held or prosecuted unless they actually harmed someone during the perpetration of the crime. Fortunately for everyone except Dad, his chomped fingers counted as harm. That was a good enough reason to hold the thief and eventually he was prosecuted for encouraging a minor to commit a crime. The minor happened to be his little brother.

In the end the thieves were taken to court, Dad's fingers were held up as evidence and in the process of investigating the crime the police found a warehouse where the thieves had stashed all of the stuff they'd stolen from the center, so we got it all back.

Word kind of spread around that Chico had been the one who caught the thieves and he basked in about one full hour of glory before we all went back to yelling at him for being so noisy.

Chapter 8

The Lake at IU

I think I've heard somewhere that we're all victims of something, which means we can blame our lives on whatever we're victims of. Well, I'm a victim of the fact that I grew up beside lakes and rivers. That's the only possible explanation for my lake at Indiana University, which had a lot of people including me quite worried.

After I graduated from Moody Bible Institute I enrolled at Indiana

University so I could get an undergraduate degree, and what I got was a whole different world. The campus was huge and gorgeous, the students were rebelliously wild and several of my professors spent a good bit of time making fun of everything I'd just learned about God and the Bible at Moody.

I remember one ethics class where we got onto the topic of religion and the prof said you couldn't trust anyone who claimed to have religious insights. I poked up my hand and disagreed.

"In the Old Testament," I argued, "the prophets were given a severe test. They had to make short term predictions along with the longer range ones and if the short ones didn't come true they got stoned."

The whole class burst out laughing. Those were the days when "stoned" meant you were on drugs and my whole point kind of got lost. That's what I mean by a whole different world.

Anyway, I started off my first year at IU on kind of the wrong foot. The problem was that I was nineteen when I started in late August, and I had never hitchhiked anywhere. There are probably a lot of you out there who wouldn't care, but to me it was an urgent thing to be approaching my 20th birthday September 15th and to realize that if I was going to hitchhike as a teenager, I only had three weeks left to do it. I'd have to skip a few classes, but I didn't think that would be a terrible thing because I had already attended plenty of classes as a teenager.

This is one of those things I never should have done, I suppose, but I didn't really think it through. I just crammed a few extra clothes in a backpack late on a Friday afternoon, grabbed a few dollars and walked to the nearest highway. Since I didn't have anyplace else to go, I'd decided to hitchhike out to Pennsylvania and visit a friend.

Well, that trip went pretty well. I didn't get stabbed or shot or beaten to death and in fact I had a lot of fun meeting people along the way and getting to know them. One really kind old man picked me up just east of Indianapolis and took me three or four hours east because he was on his way fishing. The funny thing was that on my way back he picked me up where he'd left me off three days earlier and took me right back to where we'd met in the first place. He hadn't caught any fish, but he really enjoyed me, he said.

The only close call I had on that trip was when I was trying to get my last ride on the way home. It was late at night and I was tired and when a car full of weird looking university students stopped for me, I got in without even thinking about the fact that the car smelled funny in a powerful sort of way.

We'd only gone about ten minutes when the car began drifting over to the left side of the road going 65 miles an hour, and just before we smashed into a big overpass pillar the passenger in the front suddenly lunged over and jerked the steering wheel, whipping us back into the middle of the road.

"What do you think you're doing?" he shouted at the driver using language that I just cleaned up a lot.

"I jus' wanted to see what it was like to drive with my eyes closed," the driver giggled in a kind of falsetto voice. That was how I learned what marijuana smelled like, and looking back on it I can't believe I didn't have the good sense to just get out of the car.

Anyway, my hitchhiking career took off pretty fast after that and my grades kind of didn't. I was going to northern Indiana one weekend and when I got to the bus station the bus had just left.

"Yep, leaves at 1:00 every afternoon for South Bend," said the ticket agent.

"But when I called this morning they told me 1:30," I said.

"Nope, 1:00 every afternoon," he repeated in a tone of voice that made it clear he didn't care. "But there's another one at 4:00."

I wasn't about to sit in the smoky station for three hours watching flies crawl on the ceiling, so I hiked to the highway and stuck out my thumb. Beat the bus to South Bend by 45 minutes.

I got to Chicago several times, Texas a couple of times and even California once. On the California trip my first ride was with an old gentleman who was coming back from collecting arrowheads. We had a great time together. He explained every chipped rock in the whole world and I acted so interested that he took me out for a T-bone steak and then home to meet his wife in St. Louis. She showed me her sea shell collection, which filled nearly the whole basement and was breathtakingly stunning and one of the most memorable times of my whole life, reflecting on God's creativity. They put me up for the night, fed me steak and eggs for breakfast, packed me a lunch and took me to a good spot on the highway.

The second ride was with a tired army guy who was quite happy to let me drive the whole way to Albuquerque so he could sleep. His mom was so grateful for all I'd done that she fed me supper, put me up for the night, stuffed me with a huge breakfast and took me to another good spot on the highway.

The third ride was with a hippy in a step van. The engine burned oil faster than gasoline and the steering was a bit sloppy.

We got pulled over by the police once for weaving left of center, once for leaving such a cloud of smoke and once for being suspects in a motorcycle theft.

By the third time we were pulled over my companion, who wasn't in love with the police in the first place, was genuinely mad.

"Get out of your vehicle and spread eagle," the trooper ordered in the middle of a very black night through a very loud megaphone. I, of course, instantly jumped out, spread eagled on the ground and watched my whole eventful life flash in front of my eyes.

"YOU spread eagle," the hippy shouted back. I wondered if I was going to witness an execution from a worm's eye view, and wriggled my head around on the pavement to watch. To my surprise, the police took it in stride, verified that the stolen motorcycle wasn't in the van, apologized to us and sent us on our way, wide awake and still weaving and smoking. The hippy delivered me right to the door of my California friend's house, $2.52 poorer than when I'd left IU.

I could go on, since the hitchhiking was one of the most interesting parts of my university training. I met a huge collage of the American public, spent the night in fascinating places like Lincoln Park in Chicago, ditches in Arkansas and fields all over the Midwest. I helped a lot of people get some sleep along the way, talked a lot about my faith and theirs, saw some of the country and nearly got my head whipped off by a laughing guy swinging a big antenna from the window of a car going by at 70 miles an hour. Okay, so it wasn't all fun, but most of it was.

I had a hard time getting excited about the introductory classes at IU. A lot of them were designed for people without brains, so we were packed into huge rooms where we couldn't interact or ask questions. Beyond that, I was absolutely stunned by the foolishness of some of the professors and wondered how they ever got their jobs. Just as a trivial example, one of them who happened to be a heavy smoker spent nearly a whole class period using smoking as an example of how you can't assume cause-effect from a correlation.

"Just because we see a high incidence of certain types of cancer in people who smoke," he said puffing steadily, "doesn't mean that smoking causes cancer." It occurred to me that even people in an academic community often rationalize to validate what they want to believe.

I had the same reaction to an ethics professor who spent a whole semester of my life trying to convince me and 500 other students that the only thing that would consistently give us a solid standard for our actions was our own consciences. I wished he'd just step outside his office or read the newspaper and experience a bit of what people's consciences were telling them to do in the world.

On the other hand, the university was a fabulous place to learn about all kinds of things, since there were courses on anything you could imagine. Having had the good fortune of being influenced by a high school teacher who loved to learn, I took a wide variety of classes and wished I could take more. Besides, they had every imaginable facility for recreation and diversion including a sailing club that I immediately joined. Of course I usually had to walk to the lake, which took a couple of hours, but it was worth it even on cold windy days.

I majored in anthropology, which is a sure way to lose your faith, but I didn't. My most interesting class wasn't particularly useful, but it was at least challenging. That was the "bone class," where we had to learn how to identify whole people from bits and pieces of bones.

"See that pelvis?" the prof would ask. Tell me whether it's male or female, approximately how old the person was when they died and whether they had any obvious diseases. If it's a female, did she have any children and if so, how many?

Now you might think that's all a bit like hoogy boogy, but in many cases the bones came from people who had arranged to donate their bodies to science. After they died, I mean. So the prof knew exactly what they had been like and even sometimes knew their names, which was a bit disconcerting. Anyway, he could easily tell us if we were right or wrong.

The best thing by far about IU was the fun, dedicated Christian students who got together under banners like Campus Crusade, Inter-Varsity Christian Fellowship, Navigators and the like. I developed an immense amount of admiration for some of them, who hung tough on what they believed and lived it out day by day in classrooms and dorm rooms that were stacked against them.

John Key was primary among those I got to know — a boisterous, rough and tumble, faithfully friendly guy who didn't let a whole lot get to him. He grew up surrounded by the corn fields of northern Indiana and was as interested in my weird background as I was in his. John, more than anyone else, bridged me over into life at IU. We went camping a lot in the woods near the campus and I educated him about hitchhiking, which his parents didn't particularly care for. In fact they didn't care for any of my influence on John, including the fact that he ended up going to Brazil to teach missionary kids in the jungle for a spell.

My own roommates weren't exactly role models for me. On October 31st the first one showed up in a woman's dress and strategic stuffing and makeup and informed me that he was president of the Gay and Lesbian Coalition on campus. He was also Christian Science and I couldn't quite put it all together, but then neither could he. He used to complain about the food in the cafeteria and I'd say, "You think you have it bad? I actually believe it exists."

Christian Scientists don't believe that the material world exists, but they have to pretend that it does every day of their lives or they'd get pretty hungry. When he got sick he wouldn't take any medicine, but he was quite grateful for the chicken soup I made for him, which always struck me as a little inconsistent. Anyway, I don't mind saying that it made me rather uncomfortable and self-conscious to know I had a gay roommate, and I abandoned him at the end of the semester.

The second roommate was an immature kid who brought a television and stereo with him and had them on every minute that he was awake, whether or not I was. Constantly surrounded by innane programming, thumping rock music and his steady supply of pornographic books, I quickly got a bit disillusioned about the future of our country, at least as far as he was concerned.

That's why the Christian kids meant so much to me. In such a weird world, they stood out like lights and rocks, not because they were perfect but because they cared about things that mattered.

Terry Whalin was one of the guys I really enjoyed. He was everywhere all the time — a whirlwind journalism major who'd had a pretty wild life until he committed it to Jesus Christ. That had made quite a difference and when I got to know him he was actively involved in several Christian groups on campus. I saw him one day hurrying past at a fast clip.

"Where're you going now?" I asked.

"Over to the other side of campus," he answered breathlessly.

"Here," I said, "take my bicycle. "It'll save you half an hour and I'm not going anywhere." I had a rather dilapidated 3-speed, but it worked.

"Naw," Terry said, "I like to walk." Then he hesitated, a funny look on his face.

"I've never told anyone else this," he said painfully. "My dad never taught me how to ride a bike. I still don't know how. But keep it to yourself — it's pretty embarrassing."

That's how I ended up running my legs

off, back and forth, panting and sweating and holding the bike up while Terry learned to balance. His smile after his first solo trip was worth more than gold, and one of his proudest moments was when, as a nineteen year old, he went home for Thanksgiving and rode his bike for the first time in front of his dad.

My last year I had patched up my grades enough to move into an honors dorm. There were two really good things about that small dorm: I didn't have a roommate and there were 24 Saudi Arabians on the second floor. Since it was the early seventies and OPEC was putting a stranglehold on the world oil supply, there weren't a lot of students who wanted much to do with the Saudis.

I, on the other hand, thought they were some of the more interesting people on campus, so I hung out in their rooms and even invited a couple of them to the Millers' house with me for Thanksgiving. My most memorable conversation with them had to do with the U.S. attitude toward Israel and the Arab nations. And what the Bible says about Israel. And what I thought about Israel. And did I want to die by sword or scimitar?

Actually, I didn't die by either one. We argued vehemently and ended up being very close friends. For them, the whole U.S.

experience was a chance to try new things, including ham for Thanksgiving dinner even when we specifically told them that there was plenty of turkey. And girls and beer and other things they didn't get much of at home.

The dorm was at the edge of a huge meadow that sloped down to a little stream you could step across in one stride. That stream meandered picturesquely down to an earthen bridge with a footpath across it and three culverts under it to let the stream through. I pondered that bridge and those three culverts a lot in my spare time, and found them irresistible. One very dark night I even wandered down and measured their diameter, just in case I might ever need to know.

Of course I was too broke to do anything that would cost an extra nickel, but one afternoon I happened to see some sheets of plywood discarded behind a building and thought it would be a terrible waste if I didn't squirrel them away in my room. They sat there in my way for a couple weeks until everything kind of came together one cloudy afternoon. I doubt if you could say it was providential, given the circumstances, but you might at least call it coincidental.

The weather forecast was for rain that night. A lot of rain, they thought. Buckets of rain, I hoped. I got out my jigsaw, turned up my radio for background noise and cut three big circles of plywood. Swept up the sawdust, surreptitiously got rid of the scrap plywood and waited for dark, which came early under thunderously glowering skies.

Then, as the first drops began to fall, I dressed in denim, crept across the meadow, into the creek and down to the culverts. I pressed the first circle of plywood into place, completely plugging up the culvert. Then the second. Finally the third. Then I sneaked back into the dorm, dried off and waited.

I'm not sure what I thought I would see in the morning. A big puddle? A quaint pond? A creek that had managed to push my plywood circles out of the way? I can only say that I wasn't prepared for the glorious site that met my eyes when I woke: the whole meadow had turned into an enormous lake that rose nearly to the top of the earthen bridge.

I was elated. Exhilarated. Astounded. Thrilled. Petrified.

It was still raining and the water was already lapping at the edge of the dorm across the meadow. Soon it would be inside, and my plywood plugs were under eight feet of water where I couldn't possibly get to them. I saw maintenance personnel poking and probing with flashlights, undoubtedly wondering who to kill. I saw a boat on my lake and joined a crowd of happy students at the water's edge.

"Cool," said one. "Our own lake! We could rent boats!"

"Yeah," agreed another, "and start an intramural water polo competition!"

"We can ice skate this winter," added a girl.

"Start rounding up animals two by two," laughed someone with more Bible knowledge than the average IU student.

Ideas bounced around like popcorn and I was so proud to have inspired their creativity that it was all I could do to keep from confessing. I forcibly restrained myself, of course, because it wasn't at all certain yet that I hadn't flooded the far dorm or destroyed the footpath at the end of the lake. I badly wanted the credit, but didn't at all want the blame.

Well, the rain stopped just in time and we enjoyed our lake for three whole days, swimming, playing water frisbee and canoeing. Unfortunately my plywood plugs didn't seal tightly enough and eventually the water level went down to where the maintenance guys could pull them out. There was a general atmosphere of disappointment that it wasn't more permanent and a sort of hope that whoever had done it would do it again.

"Sure wish I knew who it was," I heard more than once. "Me too," I'd say.

No one ever found out.

Chapter 9

The Land Papers

Right in the middle of a Bible study on knowing God's will for our lives, the telephone rang, interrupting us. I was with a bunch of other missionary kids in California, having hitchhiked out for a retreat at the beach. Remember the story about the arrowhead collector, the tired soldier and the hippy in the weaving, smoking step van? That trip.

Anyway, the call was for me, from my dad. Since my dad was in Peru, and since phone calls from Peru were pretty much unheard of, something serious was up. My mind raced.

"Ronny, did you hear about the Lansa crash?" I had. Christmas eve, 1971, over a hundred passengers were missing after lightning hit the plane in midair.

"They haven't found the plane yet, but they're pretty sure no one survived." Actually, they were wrong — a 12-year-old German girl landed in a tree after a long freefall and walked her way out of the jungle — one of the most remarkable survival stories ever. But they didn't know about her yet.

"You probably know that Harold Davis was in that plane along with four others from the center here, so we've been trying to think through how we're going to manage without him." Harold and Pat Davis were key partners in the Machiguenga program, working on literacy and community development projects. It was a devastating loss.

"We'd like for you to come home and help us for a few months until we can get someone else." There it was. Bottom line. Scripture translation progress in the balance and I was one of the few people who could quickly plug into the work. Dad and

Mom were pushing hard to get the New Testament translation done in rough draft — after all the years of work they were on a roll, about 2/3 of the way through and gaining speed. They didn't want to put the translation work on hold, but there were a jillion other projects that needed attention.

The Bible study was on determining God's will, so I hung up the phone, returned to the group and asked them to practice on me. Should I go, or should I not? It wasn't as easy as tearing petals off a daisy — I'd have to drop out of school and lose my own momentum.

A week later I landed at Pucallpa's rainy airport. The Lansa plane had finally been found after the lone survivor described her escape route along a jungle stream. One of the first things I did was to sit with a hundred colleagues at the memorial service.

The SIL "family" on the center was reeling. Not only had Harold died in the crash, so had four others. Nathan, a bright, promising eighth grader had just fulfilled a dream of traveling from Pucallpa to Lima by road. Roger and Margery, short-term teachers at our little school, had left their two young children at Yarinacocha with friends so they could take care of some business in Lima. David, 19, had come to Peru to visit his sister and help out however he could for a few months.

Grieving parents, orphaned children and a whole extended family wept together even as they sang songs of hope and clung to the gift of God's compassionate love in the midst of terrible tragedy and loss.

Harold had had his fingers in a dozen projects and most of his precious records were in his head or scribbled on notes that meant a lot to him but nothing to the rest of us. My first big job was to sort through them and figure out where to go next.

The most urgent project Harold had been working on was getting designated land for the Machiguengas in an attempt to protect them from outsiders who were moving into the area to log and farm. The Peruvian government was in favor of giving the Indians title to acreage around their villages, but it was still a long, tedious bureaucratic process with an uncertain outcome.

In the jungle areas, land was being allocated on a per person basis. That meant that to apply for the land, we had to know how many people lived in each village and supply a census along with the application process. The census would include names, birth dates, addresses and a few other simple things.

There were just a couple of problems. The first was that only a few of the

Machiguengas had names. They had always used a system of family relationships to keep track of each other, and I didn't think the government would be impressed by a long list that included 1,500 people called "father", another 1,500 called "mother" and the rest called "son," "daughter," "grandpa," "grandma," "aunt," "uncle" and "potential wife."

The next problem was that only a few of the Machiguengas had birthdays. I mean, they had all been born, but no one was quite sure when. It had never really mattered to them, since they could go through their whole lives without ever needing to know. When you were ready for solid foods, you ate solid foods, usually starting with something your mother chewed up and then sort of squooshed into your mouth directly from her own. When you quit piddling indiscriminately, you got pants. When you started talking, people laughed or shut you up. When you looked and acted like an adult, you got married. When you couldn't have any more children, you breathed a sigh of relief. When your body wore out, you died. Machi life in a nutshell.

I'm sure it was a real strain on grandparents since it left them with no way to brag about how early their grandchildren could bawl "gaaaaammaaaa," but there you have it. No birthdays, no comparisons, no bragging rights, no terrible trauma over delayed puberty.

Well, that would never do, so I started naming Machiguengas by the dozens as if they were my own kids and giving them birthdays as if I were God. I worked with a book of Spanish names and a group of teachers who happened to be at Yarinacocha studying.

"So who else is there in Mantaro?" I'd ask.

"My uncle," Venturo would answer. He was the teacher from Mantaro.

"How about if we call him 'Silverio'?" I'd suggest, flipping through my list of names.

"I don't think he'd like that very much," Venturo would object, as if he had any idea what his "uncle" might like for a name.

"Then how about Augusto?" After all, I couldn't use Juan or Jose for every man in the village.

"Eheh. He'll like Augusto." Augusto it was, then, not that he would know it for a while.

"How old do you think he is?" I'd continue.

"Well, he has three grandchildren," Venturo would suppose, "but he still goes hunting every day and works in his garden. He's really strong, so maybe he's around forty." Given a life expectancy of about 45 for Machiguenga men back then, Venturo was probably close.

"Let's say he was born August 15, 1932," I'd suggest, proud of myself for remembering to make the birth month actually match the name. That would make it easier for the new Augusto to remember, since his birth month would sound like his name. Not that he would remember either one of them without a lot of reminders.

On and on it went for hundreds of Machi men, women and children in a dozen villages. Sometimes when I'd suggest a name everyone would burst out laughing as if it would be preposterous to call that woman "Juana." I never figured out how to anticipate the jokes, but everyone else seemed to know when a name just didn't fit.

When everyone had been named and born, I worked with the teachers to fill out the application papers in duplicate and triplicate and umpteenlicate without the benefit of computers and copy machines.

While I worked, Jerry and Eunice Hamill joined the Machi team. Jerry was a strong, energetic diesel mechanic who could fix any machine that moved and resurrect any that didn't. He and Eunice had hearts as big as watermelons and fell in love with the Machiguengas even though they couldn't yet speak any of the language. As they let go of other duties, they began to pick up bits and pieces of the Machi work and we started talking about how to introduce them to the

Machiguenga villages. In a staff meeting one day Dad floated an idea.

"Jerry, why don't you and Ronny do a river trip? If we get a boat, you can go from village to village and kind of get acquainted along the way. It'd be the best way in the world to get a feel for how the Machis have to get around and you can visit several places without having to use the plane. Then you could go on up to Cuzco and work on the land papers from there." Cuzco was the capital of the ancient Inca empire, high in the Andes. Although it was far away and a world apart, it was still the place where the Machiguengas had to go for official business.

The boat idea was brilliant and it would nearly kill us several times. Fortunately Jerry was tall, strong and rugged. We scheduled our trip for early April, when the rivers would hopefully be going back down toward the end of the rainy season. Jerry and I would go with a Machiguenga motorist. It would be a six-week trip and I could hardly wait.

We bought a glorified 30-foot dugout canoe with a sunshade on it and added a top, canvas curtains and a 12-horse pequi-pequi engine. We named it "Adelante," which meant "Forward." There would be times when the name wasn't all that accurate, but we didn't know it then.

If you've read my first two books, you already know that a pequi-pequi is a Briggs and Stratton engine that weighs about the same as an elephant and is as loud as a machine gun in a metal storage building.

You describe pequis with words like "reliable," "hard-working," "faithful," "dependable" and "loud," sort of like my dad. But you would never hear anyone say "fast," unless maybe they were Indians who had never used anything but paddles and poles to move a canoe.

It took us a few weeks to get ready for the trip. While still working on land papers, we filled orders from the Machi school teachers for books, pencils, chalk, medicine, trade goods, shotgun shells, fish hooks, soccer shorts and a huge category of miscellaneous. All of that had to be double and triple wrapped in plastic, since we were rather sure that in spite of our best efforts, the boat would leak and rain would regularly blast past the curtains into the boat.

It's got nothing to do with anything, but I might as well interrupt my story to tell you about Art and Spanky and Nickie.

I went down to swim at the lake by our center one day and was rather taken aback to find three white skins already there. I say "skins" because that's all they were wearing. One young man, two young women. Peace children, lovers of the earth, back to nature, fruit and berries kind of people. They were quite happy to have me join them, but since I was having a bit of trouble keeping my eyes in the right places I decided against it. We chatted briefly and then I went to let the center director know that he might want to look into the situation.

It turned out that the three were hippies who had set up camp across the lake and were living off "God's provision," which mainly meant the neighbor's fruit trees. They weren't in the best of health, partly because God's provision was giving them chronic diarrhea and partly because they didn't have any idea how to sterilize water, food or themselves, other than their daily dip in the lake.

Having real hippies on our center was about as exciting as if a trio of jaguars had suddenly walked through. Tongues wagged and people gravitated either toward the group that were disgusted with them for their loose and filthy lives or toward the group that saw them as just another kind of people who lived differently than we did and needed the true love of God to touch their lives.

I was in the second group and had had a lot of contact with hippies both in Chicago and at Indiana University, so I took the rather radical step of befriending them. My parents were genuinely interested in them as well, so they got the wonderful pleasure of our shower and real meals periodically. Eventually they even moved into the detached apartment behind our house, with Nickie's two young children in tow.

There's a lot I could say about those three, and some of it would even be complimentary. Behind the loose morals and looser clothes they were kind, generous, loving people looking for some sort of meaning in life. Though we couldn't possibly have foreseen it at the time, Spanky wrote to us years later to say that she had decided to turn her life over to Jesus Christ and had become a missionary herself. She wanted to thank us for our influence back when she was searching in all the wrong places.

On a cloudy, windy morning Art and Spanky helped us load the boat while our friend Ruth Curran, who was in Peru as a short-term helper, frantically finished typing the land papers. The boat sank dangerously low in the water, so while Jerry and I ate lunch, Dad and the Machis took off about 250 pounds of gear. Then a loud whistle blew on the center and friends and colleagues streamed to the shore of the lake to pray for us and wave us off. Just as I got ready to step onto the bow of the boat, Art handed me a home-made bracelet and wished me well.

Miguel, our motorist, was a short, handsome Machi friend about my age who I'd known since we were both little boys. He headed us off into a brisk southern wind that whipped the lake into whitecaps that slapped hard against our bow. To steer, he held onto a three-foot long, thick iron bar that stuck out in front of the engine. The engine had an eight-foot tail attached to the back of it with a propeller at the end. It was all balanced on a thick pin that allowed it to swivel in all directions and even up and down in case of shallow water or logs. The design was ingeniously practical even though it took a good bit of practice to get good at working it. I've seen rookies get thrown right out of the canoe by an engine that got mischievous.

By the time we entered the narrow channel to the Ucayali River twenty minutes later, we were soaked from the spray, were bailing the boat regularly and were wondering just how we'd ever make it through the dozens of rapids far upriver.

In the channel, thick jungle sheltered us from the wind. High green branches arched over us protectively and birds fluttered up in front of our noisy boat. It was a brief step back into tropical paradise, but it didn't last long enough. When we exited it an hour later into the wide river just below Pucallpa we immediately knew we were in for a workout.

The Ucayali, one of the two main tributaries of the Amason, was in an unseasonal high flood stage, its churning brown waters filled with fallen trees. Everywhere along the banks we could see houses on stilts completely surrounded by water. We had to cross the river and it took us a full 45 minutes, trying to hold our own against the current while we dodged logs and other boats. When we reached the other side, we were down river from where we had started and I was dismayed. At this rate, the only way we'd ever get to the Machiguenga area would be by going backwards around the world.

Late the first afternoon there was almost no land in sight. In the burnt red light of a stunning sunset, we tied up at a small patch of mud and feasted on fried chicken and rolls and fudge from home while mosquitoes feasted on us. We tried to sleep, but it was pretty sketchy and by 2:30 in the morning we decided we were wasting our time. I pushed us off the mud and huddled on the bow in a persistent drizzle to help Miguel watch for logs by the light of an intermittent moon. We ran out of gas just before dawn and lost half a mile by the time we could refuel.

There was only one way to make any progress up the river, and that was to stay close to the bank where shoreline obstacles and small backwaters slowed down the current. We hugged it so closely that for most of the next week we could reach out at any time and touch overhanging branches. We all became experts at watching for submerged logs and small sandbars just under the surface, and although I can't say it was exhilarating, our progress was steady. Any time we had to cross the river, we ended up farther down river than we'd been when we started across.

I kept a journal of the next nine days, but you wouldn't find it fascinating. Slogging upriver is a long and tedious chore interrupted unpredictably by moments of sheer panic. For nearly half of every night and all day long we listened to the head-splitting noise of the pequi as we took turns driving, sleeping and watching the jungle subtly change from the flat lowlands of the Amazon basin to the rumply foothills of the Urubamba River valley. Rain storms plastered us daily, sometimes in driving sheets that blasted right through our curtains and sometimes in depressing drizzles that chilled us to the bone hour after hour.

Late every afternoon we searched for some place to tie up for the night. Once it was in an abandoned house up to its knees in muddy water and swarming with bats and mosquitoes. With the river running just under the palm floor, we had a sink, a flush toilet and a five-minute rain shower within easy reach. Twice we tied up to logs stuck in the middle of the river. Other boats tied onto us and then each other until there was a chain of boats depending on our rope. In one boat there was an old man who begged us to pull a tooth that was driving him crazy, but we hadn't come prepared with dental equipment.

Once we even found a small sand bar where I sacked out under the stars until I heard a twig snap by my head and spun around, frightening something that raced back into the jungle. In the morning, in the sand, there were big cat tracks around my bed.

Mosquitoes were a constant problem the first few days, to the point where we thought some nights about just putting a cup of blood on the bow of the boat to make it easier for them. Our nets weren't easy to put up in the boat and mosquitoes easily found their way in. We usually pushed off in the middle of the night just to get away from them and then had some of our closest calls running into logs in the dark.

The further we got upriver, the faster the current got. We snuggled up to the shore and looked for any way to avoid the strongest part of the current. At times the cross currents and backwaters clashed violently with the main current. Sometimes we would cruise upstream in a backwater only to hit the main current so hard that the bow would rise a foot and water would come in over the back of the canoe while we frantically hung onto the tiller to try and keep the boat pointed in the right direction.

Day six we swung into a narrow channel away from the main part of the river. The current got faster and faster as we approached the upper end where there was a huge log jam. We were creeping along the left bank when a cross-current threw us toward shore. I grabbed a paddle to help Miguel, but it was too late. We hit a log that had been supporting another log. The top one crashed down onto the side of the boat and pinned us, radically tipped to the left side. Jerry and I heaved on the log with all our might and got the boat partly out from under the log, but that made it tip even further so that we started taking in water over the edge.

Miguel and Jerry scrambled to the right side while I continued to strain against the log's weight. With a desperate heave I lifted the log and as the current pushed us out from under it the boat tipped back to the right so violently that Jerry and Miguel were nearly thrown overboard. The bow swung into the current, the tail on the engine got jammed against a log and Miguel bent the steel bar trying to regain control.

Day seven we turned off the Ucayali and into the Urubamba River, the boiling heart of my homeland. My blood also boiled with a mixture of anticipation and apprehension. The Urubamba was smaller and wilder, with over 70 fast rapids between us and the first Machi village. High red cliffs often guarded the river, interspersed with long sand bars. Wicked cross currents could easily grab the front of the boat and overpower the motorist, who didn't have much leverage on the engine.

Late in the afternoon that day we entered an innocent looking channel, Jerry at the helm. At the upper end of the channel there was a rapid too fast for the engine, so I gave Jerry some instructions and Miguel and I grabbed long cane poles to help push us forward against the current. Inch by inch we groped our way up until we were ready to hit the main current, running perpendicular to us. Jerry would have to get us turned at the last instant so we'd hit it head on instead of sideways. Otherwise we'd get spun around and slam into a massive log jam where the water raged and churned.

In a split second we spun around, Jerry

straining so hard against the tiller that he bent it again. I looked back and he was a burly bundle of sweat and terror. We smashed sideways into the logs, tipped precariously and lost our poles. Miguel and I clutched at logs to try and slow us down, and then Miguel just jumped off with our bow rope and whipped it around a sturdy tree. Unfortunately when the boat hit the end of the slack the rope just broke right off the bow and Miguel was left standing on his log with the rope in his hand. It was so funny I had to take a moment to burst out laughing even as I paddled furiously toward shore. Jerry wasn't laughing. We were on our own now, racing back down river with a stalled engine.

We finally got the engine started, collected Miguel and went back down around to the main river. By now the engine wasn't happy — it kept quitting at the most awkward times and Jerry, who was new to all of this, was having a tough time with sheer panic whenever it quit. I tried to calm him down with thoughts about how little danger there really was if it quit for a few seconds, but actually it was hard to ignore the boiling rapids just down river from us. If we had drifted back into them without engine power, they would have sunk us in an instant.

It got even worse the next day, when we

discovered we'd lost our only paddle in the night. And worse yet when we discovered our engine had blown a head gasket and the nearest parts stores were back in Pucallpa, now 300 miles away by river.

When the engine died, Jerry came alive. We drifted back to a sand bar and he took it apart for a look. He removed the old gasket, stuffed it with some kind of magic gookum and said a prayer. It started and ran, which would make Jerry famous in Machi country for a long time to come. Of course the other thing that would make him famous would be the time he decided to piddle with one foot on the bow and the other on the bank and the boat drifted away, dumping him in the river with his dignity severely shaken. The Machis called him "The Piddling One" when Miguel told them the story but I'm sure he'd rather have been called "The Engine Fixing One."

Next it was a spark plug wire that let go in the middle of a ferocious rapid and then a rich/lean mixture screw, all of which Jerry fixed with a quickness and sureness that amazed me. If I'd been alone, I think I'd have just thrown the engine overboard.

I had been reading through the Old Testament along the way and was impressed by the saga of the Israelites' journeys through the wilderness as compared to our own. It was easy to relate to them, having serious doubts right after you've had very clear indications that God is on your side.

Day nine we motored through a torrential downpour that left the banks glistening with waterfalls. I poled steadily to help out the engine and to keep myself warm against the wet wind. Around noon we finally pulled up to the high bank in front of Nueva Luz, climbed up to the village and greeted a welcoming crowd of familiar faces. I was home.

Jerry wasn't home. He looked a little like a fish in the desert — it's one thing to love the people in general and quite another to love so many individuals so suddenly. I taught him how to say "Are you?" to each and every individual, and then told the people that one of the best things about Jerry was that he could fix things. Immediately a broken radio showed up and Jerry made himself forever famous by fixing it on the spot.

As we visited around the village I scattered cooking bananas in my "mothers'" and "sisters'" cook fires, then returned to collect them later, toasty brown with crisp outsides and hot moist insides. Though we had a long list of business items to take care of, for a couple of hours it was enough just to taste the delicious sensation of being back with family.

Chapter 10

Cristobal and Carmen

Things in our hut in were a colossal mess. Bits and pieces of three 10-horse Briggs and Stratton engines covered a quarter of the floor like a junkyard while Jerry the master mechanic tried to resurrect one healthy pequi-pequi boat engine out of three dead ones. Scattered around the rest of the hut were 75 dried skins from pigs, jaguars and otters, damp clothes and bedding that hung from ropes and poles, leftover food from two weeks of river travel, boxes of books, dirty dishes, egg shells, papaya peelings and more. In a nutshell, it wasn't pretty and my mother wouldn't have been proud.

It was 5:30 in the afternoon. Somehow this entire mess would have to be cleaned up, packed up and ready to move by the next morning. It was going to be a long night and we were already too tired to think straight.

I was dabbling with the packing when Navidad suddenly showed up beside the porch. Navidad has been one of my favorite people ever since the days when I was his reading teacher. He never learned how to read, but he appreciated my efforts and we were "brothers," according to Machi reckoning, even though he was quite a bit older than me. He wore a tattered baseball cap sort of twisted to one side of his head. Come to think of it, I don't ever remember seeing him without that cap — maybe he was born with it stuck to his hair and it just sort of grew up with him like ears and toenails do.

Navidad was also one of the most mature Christian men I knew. He was quiet, humble and kind and had a bashful sense of humor, always putting a hand over his mouth when he laughed. He had a few scraggly bits of beard and tattered clothes. I figured he'd just come to hang out with us for a while and watch us bundle the skins

174

and the rest of our junk.

"Are you?" I greeted him and he answered with a smile, "I am." Reassured once again that he was instead of wasn't, which would have been a bit ghostly, I offered him a mat and invited him to have a seat.

He sat soberly for a while, making small talk and just watching. Not edgy, not in a rush, not particularly concerned. In fact, when he got to the point of his business, his request just slipped out like your shirt tail might come untucked without you even noticing it.

"Would you and Jerry come see Cristobal? He's dying."

I'd known Cristobal and his wife Carmen for as long as I could remember. He was a tall scrawny man with high cheekbones and a wide mouth and wild hair. He'd suffered from severe tuberculosis and pretty much any other disease that the jungle had to offer recently. Carmen was a beautiful woman in every way, with long black hair and a gorgeous smile. They lived away from the main part of the village pretty close to where Navidad's house was. Apparently Cristobal had taken a turn for the worse. I mean, dying could hardly be described as an improvement.

Jerry and I dropped everything and followed Navidad across the end of the airstrip, through a short stretch of jungle, into Cristobal and Carmen's clearing. We bent way over and ducked our heads to get through the doorway, waited a few moments to let our eyes adjust to the dim light of a tiny kerosene lamp made out of a coffee can.

The thatched roof, glistening black from years of cookfire smoke, was so low that we couldn't straighten up and we wished for the zillionth time that we were as short as the Machis. There were no windows in this house, just cane walls all the way around. It wouldn't have mattered anyway — by the time we got there the sun had set and darkness had rushed in to fill every nook and cranny of the jungle.

"You've come," murmered Carmen.

"We've come," we each whispered back.

Cristobal lay on a platform of hard cane poles with no mattress or pad. Carmen stood beside him, strikingly pretty even here, wearing her cushma. Behind them a few neighbors squatted silently on the dirt floor, waiting for him to die, waiting to see what we would do about it.

Jerry quietly asked me questions and I translated them as best as I could while I felt various parts of Critobal. Pulse too weak to find, face ashen, breathing rattly and strained. Legs and arms cold to the touch. So cold that I kind of jerked back when I touched them, in fact. Skin on ankles and knees cracked and peeling off, like rotten leather. No fever that I could feel, no nausea, according to Carmen. Fierce pain in the side of his head and in fact general pain all over. A village health promotor with basic medical training had given him two penicillin shots the week before, but they hadn't done any good.

Of course we wanted to help, but there wasn't much we could do. There are times when you'd really like to heal with a touch, to make everything better instantly, to be able to resurrect bodies instead of engines.

"We'll talk to the doctor by radio first thing tomorrow morning," I told them. Our doctor at Yarinacocha was the closest thing we had to a miracle worker.

"He'll be dead by then," said Navidad, and although it sounded terribly inconsiderate to say so in front of Carmen, we all suspected it was true.

Cristobal was restless and wanted to sit up. Carmen gently lifted and held him as he tried to talk, but nothing intelligible would come out. No one helped her hold him, including me. In fact, I would happily have just run away from the whole hopeless situation, since there wasn't anything I could do about it and just sitting there seemed rather pointless. There wasn't even anything much to be said, though I sort of wished I could think of something that would be meaningful. In the end we just sat with the rest for a few minutes, then got up to go.

"Let us know if anything changes," we said. Then we crouched back through the doorway, stumbled in pure blackness through the jungle, stared up at glittery stars while we crossed the end of the airstrip. Once home we lit our gas lantern and I whipped together a supper of fruit salad and fried eggs, which did nothing to take our minds off Cristobal. Nor did our frantic packing and it was no big surprise when Navidad's little son and daughter materialized out of the darkness.

"He's dead."

"He's dead?"

"Uh huh."

They waited for us to grab flashlights, then led the way back to the hut. On the way I couldn't get Carmen out of my mind: fifteen minutes ago a poised, pretty, faithful wife, her arm around her dying husband's shoulders. Now, suddenly, a lonely widow.

When we ducked into the hut, the scene was frozen as we'd last seen it. The neighbors still squatted against the back wall, Carmen stood near Cristobal's head, Cristobal himself lay eerily still, no longer wheezing and rattling. No one showed any more emotion than Cristobal did, which was a bit disconcerting.

I asked Navidad to join me outside so he

could tell me what to do next. He explained
the burial process: wrapping the body in a
woven mat with Cristobal's clothes and
other personal belongings, tying the ends
shut with a vine, taking the body downriver
to a sandbar — all things I'd done before
and didn't particularly want to do again.

"If we don't bury him," Navidad said,
"Carmen will have to do it herself. No one
else will help her." He didn't need to remind
me that everyone else would be too afraid of
Cristobal's spirit to want to handle the dead
body. It was nothing short of miraculous
that he himself was willing to help out. As
I said, his faith in God made a genuine
difference in his life.

"I'll go with you in the morning," I said.
"We'll put an engine together so we can get
there faster. Just send your children for me
when you're ready." I went back inside briefly
to say goodbye to Carmen, wishing I knew of
something comforting to say and knowing
full well that there wasn't anything. I hoped
she could see in my eyes that I cared,
although in the dim light I suspected it was
pretty hard to see my eyes at all.

Jerry and I went back to the hut, put the
engine together and slept briefly before
little Miguel came to get me at 5:30. I
slipped on jeans and a T-shirt, both damp
from the early morning fog that had
penetrated the hut. We carried the engine

down a narrow path to the port, where the mat-wrapped body lay in the bow of the dugout canoe. It looked more like a torpedo than a casket and was tied to a carrying pole that made it look even more like a bundle of bananas, manioc or firewood.

Carmen perched forlornly on the side of the canoe, her arms tucked into her robe as she tried to seal out the damp chill. She looked completely alone. I wanted to put my arms around her shoulders as she had done for her husband, but I worried that it would make her self-conscious, so I kept my sadness inside and she kept hers.

For five minutes the engine blasted down the Urubamba River like a machine gun, bringing us to a good burial spot. We tied up the canoe and Navidad cut away vines and branches while I started digging. It went fast, but soon we were both sweating from the exertion as we went deeper and deeper. Navidad wanted to be sure that the jaguars wouldn't be able to dig up the body.

Over our heads and all around us the jungle was coming to raucous life. Birds squawked irreverently. Crickets shrilled love sounds to each other. Dew drops dripped from a million leaves as Navidad finished the digging.

"Ario," he said briefly, using a kind of short hand for "that's good enough so let's get this over with." We went back down to the canoe for the body, each shouldering one end of the carrying pole. Cristobal dangled between us, heavily resting in peace as we struggled up the steep bank, Navidad in the front and me in the back. It was so steep, in fact, that at one point the whole bundle slid down the pole toward me and I had to grab a stiffly wrapped foot to keep Cristobal from kicking me in the stomach, which didn't have a whole lot of appeal.

The hole we'd dug was just long enough for the body bundle. We laid the carrying pole lengthwise across it so that the ends of the pole rested on the sand and the mat hung over the hole. Navidad picked up his machete and without hesitation or ceremony cut the vines that held the bundle to the pole. The machete rang and with a loud clatter of dishes and cooking pots and a heavy thud, Cristobal's body hit the bottom of the hole. Even though my mind knew that he wouldn't feel anything, I winced for him. I noticed out of the corner of my eye that Carmen's face didn't even twitch.

I thought we should do something like sing a song or say a prayer, but Navidad was in a hurry now to be finished. He handed me the shovel so I could start filling sand back into the hole. Carmen waited patiently, one arm wrapped around her chest to hold her robe close, the other under her chin. If we did the job right, in a few weeks there would be no sign that we had ever been there.

"Ario," Navidad said again and we went back to the canoe. He drove, I sat in the middle of the canoe and Carmen sat on the left side toward the front for the longer ride back upriver. Her face and body were quiet, but I watched big tears slowly run down her cheeks, off her chin, into her lap. I had never lost anyone close to me and hadn't a clue what it meant to no longer have a familiar companion, the father of my children, the hunter and fisher of my meat. Although I always loved to be on the river in the early morning, this time I ached, discreetly watching my sister.

When we got back to the village, we tied up the canoe and walked slowly up the bank. I said I would have to go get ready to leave. They said okay, and I knew that even though they would never say thank you, they were grateful. As I walked away I heard Navidad talking in a tender, gentle voice to Carmen about Cristobal. About his faith in God. About his new home where he wouldn't suffer. About how God would take care of her.

There is a time and a place and a way to say it. I still had a lot to learn, and even then I would never be a Machiguenga.

Chapter 11

The Truck Ride

Sunday a low fog blew through the hut where Jerry and I had spent the night. I creaked out of my mosquito net, picked up damp bedding and jumped off the porch to look for a place where I could dry them. The Machis quietly watched me struggle to arrange my soggy sheet and blanket on the thatched roof of the chicken house. It took a while, what with the fact that there was a chilly breeze and I was trying to keep everything clean as I flung it up and over. When I was done, they matter-of-factly told me there was a clothesline behind the house. Typical.

We spent the day casually, worshiping with the Machis and laughing to ourselves about their singing, feasting on chicken soup and bananas for lunch, examining a sick lady who fortunately didn't know how little we knew. In the afternoon we would have a village meeting to discuss land papers and agricultural projects. In preparation, I looked over the notes we'd written up about what we hoped to accomplish in each village we visited. It was a long list.

1. "Meet key figures. Who is the village leader? Who is the teacher? Who is the leader of the agricultural project? Does he have a book for keeping records? Does he know how to use his book?"

We were working at a pretty basic level here and couldn't assume that the leader of the ag project could read and write, even if he did have a notebook. We couldn't even assume that he knew there was an ag project or that he was its leader.

Elected leaders were a pretty recent idea. In one village Dad emphasized over and over that the election had to be kept secret, so when the "clerk" collected the ballots he counted them and then ate them, one by one.

2. "Check store and meet store keepers. Inventory? Cash on hand? Bookkeeping procedures? How much out on credit? Problems?"

Well, there were plenty of problems, all right. Theoretically the bookkeeping was done in books, which is how it got its name. In reality, the Machis found it a lot more convenient to keep everything in their heads, which made it a little hard to audit. And as to the credit issue — they'd been advised endlessly to never extend credit, but most of what they sold was on credit or traded for eggs, fruit, pig skins, necklaces or handbags. Cash on hand was almost always less than I keep in my penny jar at home.

Jerry spent a whole afternoon with the storekeeper in Nueva Luz dealing with these problems. That night the confused man pulled me aside under cover of darkness and asked me, "Am I supposed to be making money at my store?" Like I said, there were plenty of problems.

3. "Meet health promotors. Inventory. Cash on hand. Bookkeeping procedures. How much out on credit? Receive clinic reports. Check village for severe cases. Check his technique (unobtrusively). Problems?"

Of course the same problems applied, with the additional one of trying to check a health promotor's technique unobtrusively. I mean, what were we supposed to do, hide behind a tree while they took someone's temperature? Or put a cushma over our heads while they palpated someone's liver? I don't think we did too good of a job on that one.

4. "Check agricultural program. Has a bean or peanut project been started? If not, when will it start? Collect list of men who are participating. Is seed on hand? If not, find a source. Advise people that a boat is purchased and arrangements will be made to take all of their produce to Pucallpa after the first of the year. NOTHING IS TO BE SOLD UNTIL THEN and NOTHING IS TO BE SOLD THROUGH OTHER CHANNELS.

This was the crucial part of our trip. The Machiguengas hadn't ever really cooperated on anything, but they needed to. River traders took advantage of them by paying individuals peanuts for their peanuts, when a joint effort would allow them to hold out for higher prices. If only we could get them to work together and sell together, they would profit together. Unfortunately it's a pretty ingrained part of Machi life to not trust anyone else, and especially to not trust anyone who is a leader.

Well, our "to-do" list went on for 14 pages, broken down by villages and individuals. It was a monstrous job that included collecting animal hides from stores and clinics, taking orders for goods and medicines, dispersing money to various people who'd earned it one way or another, checking on sick people, selling fish line, fixing guns, lanterns, sewing machines, motors and radios, seeing if there were adequate school books, verifying fuel supplies for the airplanes, delivering salt, encouraging the people to build latrines and even measuring the height of the front wheels on the home made mowing machine in Camisea.

Some of these things could be dealt with at the community meetings, and one was coming up at 4:00 in Pablo's house. Pablo was the storekeeper — the one who asked me if he should be making money at his store.

Mariano blew a long blast on a cow's horn and jolted me out of a peaceful Sunday afternoon nap. Jerry and I wandered down to Pablo's house and waited for an hour or so for everyone else to arrive, which was pretty typical. The school teacher apologetically explained that the people were sort of independent renegades who did things at their own pace and didn't particularly like being told what to do. I decided to keep that in mind when it was my turn to talk to them.

In the dim light of a gasoline lantern I introduced the concept of the ag project:

they would clear land together, plant together, harvest together, sell together and reap the benefits on a shared basis. They would have more clout, they would get more money, they could move ahead. It would help their community pull together and make progress. It was a brilliant solution to some of their problems and not a bad presentation on my part, I thought.

I was talking in a mixture of Spanish and Machiguenga to a stony audience that wasn't moved by my enthusiasm. No standing ovations. No ovations at all. Not even polite grunts.

The problem with the Machiguengas was that they weren't ignorant savages nor noble savages nor savages at all. Just real people like you and me, who had a pretty clear idea of what they wanted in life but sometimes not so clear an idea of how to get it. They were experts at hunting and gathering and planting gardens in the jungle but not so expert at interacting with the outside world, nor at figuring out how to pay for things they desperately wanted like clothes, cooking pots, medicines, machetes and school books.

Sometimes Machis actually worked together for the greater good, sometimes they were clearly self centered. Sometimes they talked openly in meetings, sometimes they sat or squatted quietly for hours on end. Sometimes they honored their village leaders, sometimes they criticized them mercilessly. Sometimes the leaders led, other times they just used their authority to get rich and powerful.

In this meeting, my ideas weren't exactly making the Machi men giddy with excitement. I sat down so they could discuss the whole concept and got a little taste of what my parents and the Davises had endured over the years. They didn't want to work on a community project, they said. They wanted to each work their own land. There wasn't enough money in it. Who would be the leader? Where would they plant the beans and rice and peanuts? What if it didn't work. On and on for two hours, back and forth over the same ground.

It was crucial that they take as long as they needed to buy into the project, but there were times when I wanted to jump up and shout, "Look, do you want cookpots and cortisone cream or don't you? You haven't had 'em for 2,000 years and you won't get 'em by letting outsiders just rip you off at every opportunity, so why don't you at least give it a good try?"

Fortunately I didn't jump up and shout, nor did anyone else. It was more like a low grade murmur with occasional comments that surfaced to the whole group. In the end Pablo himself got frustrated and asked for a show of hands of all those who would join the cooperative effort. A few hands went up with apparent conviction and couple more that looked like maybe someone was just stretching. They appointed a provisional leader and we moved on to the land papers.

After all the work Harold and I had done on land papers, it would have been nice to just get a solid round of applause when I told them all we had done. I explained that we had a name and a birthdate for everyone, which we would give them the next day, and that we were on our way to Quillabamba and Cuzco to file the papers. They would get so many acres per person and everyone would live happily ever after, I thought.

"We don't want this land," said one of my uncles. "It's no good."

There was a long pause, which is hard to write into a story. If you like, you can just stop reading for about two minutes and let it all soak in — four months of work, nine days of exhausting boat trip, dim light, cold audience. Imagine, if you like, what you would say next. I mean, if this land was no good, why had they chosen to live there for the last 10 years?

"Then you'll have to tell me clearly what land you do want," I said, "so I can tell them in Cuzco." Thank God I don't have a quick temper — something the Machis themselves had taught me.

For the next hour we went round and round on the land issues with them interrupting each other and muttering to themselves and disagreeing back and forth so quietly that I missed a lot of it. Jerry was completely in the dark but could at least tell that if they thought this was a fabulous idea they were very good at not showing it.

In the end, they said they'd accept this land. Everyone said *"ario,"* the equivalent of "that's it, then," and we were done. I was done in. It didn't help that I hadn't a clue if we had accomplished anything, since it's one thing to raise your hand in a meeting and quite another to actually get out and clear land with your neighbor. But at least we'd made a start.

Well, we moved from village to village going through the same things over and over, passing out medicines and school books and names and birthdates. It was up to the school teachers to keep reminding everyone what their name was until it finally soaked in.

The most excitement we had along the way was the afternoon when we were lazily motoring up the Picha River on our way to Huallana. Suddenly Jerry shouted at me to look up from the book I was reading. In front of us a deer stood in shallow water, ignoring our approach.

Our motorist, Abel, immediately grabbed for his shotgun, seeing only supper, and sent off a volley that completely missed. The noise scared another deer out of the jungle. It clattered across the rocky beach as we pulled up to shore and I leaped out with a machete in my hand. Abel yelled that a third one was coming my way and I got within 10 feet of it before it veered off. Then we saw a fourth, about half grown, hiding in some sawgrass.

Abel and I took off after the young one, running. It headed for the river, plunged in and started to swim across. Abel gave up, but I stripped down to my shorts and dived in after it, swimming my heart out. When I caught up, I tried grabbing it but got kicked. Tried again and got kicked again. Finally went for its head and it went under, but by now it was confused, so it turned around and headed back to where Abel could grab it from the boat while Jerry drove

We took our catch ashore for pictures, but had to recatch it with flying tackles several more times when it struggled loose. Finally Abel took it back to the boat and tied it up, alive and bawling and as the adrenaline wore off I wished it had gotten away. To the Machis it would just be a hunk of precious meat, but to me, suddenly, it was a pet. There's a world of difference, and one that my friends would never understand as they ate it.

Our final village was Camisea, where we had planned for a plane to pick us up and take us to an airstrip far upriver. Three more people from Yarinacocha would join us for that part of the trip—Ruth and Joyce and Neal. Ruth had come to Peru several times to help with technical typing and other secretarial work. Joyce was a friend of hers and Neal was Pat Davis' 12-year-old son, whom Jerry had invited to join us. Together we would all head for Cuzco by plane, boat and truck.

Well, I could spend whole chapters on the plane, boat and truck bit. Along the way we visited my favorite sister Antonina, who was being accused of poisoning a man from upriver with strychnine. I got all the details and told her we'd check in with her attorney in Quillabamba. And we had an adrenaline rush riding in a river launch through some of the biggest rapids on the Urubamba. And we ended up in the little city of Quillabamba looking for a way to continue on to Cuzco, capital of the old Inca empire and seat of the government in that province.

Quite unexpectedly around noon we came across a truck headed for Cuzco. It was a mid-sized Ford 600 that was already half full of cargo, but the driver said we could all pile in with the 30 other passengers already on board. Well, it looked a bit crowded, with no good places to actually sit, but since it was the only thing going we climbed in.

In a massive cloud of dust we bounced off, not particularly comfortable but at least moving. The majority of our fellow travelers were Quechua women on their way to market, each taking a huge bundle of produce or weavings. We'd been going a whole ten minutes when the driver pulled over in a small stream so his helper could wash the truck. I guess it hadn't occurred to him to wash it before we all got in. We all waited semi-patiently, then smiled happily in English and Quechua when we took off again.

Thirty minutes later we crossed a slightly larger stream, pulled off to the side and waited while the helper washed the truck again. "At this rate," I thought, "we'll die of old age before we get to Cuzco, but at least we'll die in a clean truck.

As we got further from Quillabamba we stopped for more and more people who needed a ride. Each clambered in with a huge bag that couldn't be sat on or a chicken that had to be watered every hour or a stalk of bananas that were definitely fragile. People were on top of cargo and on top of other people, shouting if they were getting buried and laughing if they were burying someone else.

About 3:00 a shriveled old man in raggedy

clothes climbed in with a huge bundle and his own stalk of bananas. He immediately became a bouncing ping pong ball. Robust women pushed him back and forth as he landed on them, or kicked and cursed him. One powerful woman beat on him with her fist, others stole his bananas as he lurched, but he wasn't about to give in. He stubbornly balanced his bundle and remaining bananas right on top of someone else's baggage and plunked himself down on a woman's head.

The five of us gringos scrunched up against one wall of the truck, flat as pancakes, and enjoyed what we could see of the scenery. Neal was getting the worst of it-he was just too small to contend with the avalanches of women and baggage that buried him and twisted him into obviously uncomfortable shapes. He muttered and mumbled and flailed with his fists, but most of the women had on multiple layers of skirts and didn't even feel his hammerings. For most of the trip, all we could see of Neal was his blonde hair and hat.

4:30 came about a week later. We passed another truck that had broken down beside the road and our driver ignoring the deafening noise of sixty protesting passengers, stopped to pick up ten more with all of their baggage. Although we were close to being suffocated, we all burst out laughing. One bundle that came over the rails was three and a half feet in diameter and it stayed airborne for a full two minutes as hands shoved it this way and that. The level of humanity rose four more feet and body odor covered us like a fog.

It was 6:00 before an impending mutiny forced the driver to quit picking up more people. One man kept yelling at his daughter, "Don't move, Nellie, stay right where you are." I had to laugh. All we could see of Nellie was a hat and two braids and it would have taken a backhoe to move her. I didn't know how she could even breathe!

As the sun set, a snow-capped peak caught it's silvery light-a glowing, breathtaking end to the day. We were climbing steadily toward the snow line by now, leaving behind the jungle and grinding into cactus and eucalyptus. The air got crisp and dry and cold and we wondered how we would ever find our warm clothes, buried far below in the pre-Cambrian layer of the truck.

Fortunately, the Civil Guard and local narcotics agents solved our problem. About the time we thought we'd never be able to move again, we were told to pull over for an inspection. Everyone had to get out, which was sort of a matter of excavating us layer by layer. Then our baggage had to come off so the C.G. could search for drugs. Not that it was a very thorough search—it didn't take an inspector with a magnifying glass to see that we had twenty or thirty huge burlap bags full of cocaine leaves on the truck. In the middle of the inspection I plunged into the bowels of the truck to retrieve our bags and we pulled on welcome sweat shirts, sweaters and jackets.

I talked with the driver while the narco agents were hunting for something besides the bags of cocaine leaves, which apparently didn't count. He gave me the discouraging news that this would be an all night trip, so we might as well be prepared. We all bought bowls of soup and bottles of soda pop and stretched as if we might never move again.

Somehow when we got back into the truck we five had lost a lot of ground, but we weren't the only ones. One angry man tromped right over the top of people, stepping on them while he tried to find a place to land. He shouted at someone who had taken his place, yelled at the driver for a while, then grabbed his bundle and jumped off. He'd wait for the next truck, he said.

Four hours later we topped out on a high pass around 15,000 feet. Stars glittered just out of reach. Under a brilliant moon, snow capped peaks glowed with a soft white light. Fortunately it was beautiful, because we would have a long opportunity to enjoy it.

The driver chose that spot for his night's sleep. As a bitter cold permeated our every pore and we gasped for oxygen, he snored in the cab, oblivious to our discomfort. Some of the Quechuas, used to the cold and the altitude, slept along with him, but most of us couldn't begin to get comfortable enough for sleep. We lifted Neil out of his spot for a stretch and he got shoved around until finally a big old Quechua woman let him land on her. He fell asleep with his face against her chest, one long black braid hanging down over his blonde hair and her wrinkled, weather-beaten cheek against his head.

About 2:00 in the morning our fellow passengers had had all they could stand. They started banging on the cab, eventually bringing the driver back to reality with a really sour look on his face. We started moving again, this time descending quickly. Explosive backfiring from the truck echoed off the mountainsides and reverberated into the valleys. For four more hours we wound slowly down switchbacks until finally, just as the sun came up, we pulled into the central market in Cuzco.

Sixty five of us slowly came back to life like dead grass after a rain. We were wrinkled and covered with dust and smelled like rotten bananas dipped in sweat and chicken droppings. All in all, I'd have to say it was one of the best trips I've ever had.

Chapter 12

Sandy's Gift

You're in luck. None of us can remember how this story started, so you don't have to read the first half. Just take my word for it that Sandy and I weren't born in Cuzco, so we had to have gotten there somehow. It was probably one of those terrible trips that we've purposely repressed.

Ruth, Joyce, Neal, Jerry and I got back to Yarinacocha from our trip just in time for my sister Sandy's graduation from high school. It was very touching and memorable, but I don't remember anything about it. What I DO remember is offering her a trip for her graduation gift. I needed to go back to Cuzco to work on Machi land papers anyway, so it was actually cheaper that buying her something.

I'm still not sure why she would accept my offer. Just the year before I had returned to Peru for the summer, with a 6-man rubber raft severely stretching my baggage allowance. I took my friend Tim "Towner" Townsend and Sandy on a 14-day float from high on the Urubamba River clear down to Pucallpa. Sandy only remembers a couple of things about that trip and I'm sure she's exaggerating about both of them.

"I remember that you always put me in the front of the raft," she said severely, "so I got all the spray from the big waves and I was icy cold all the time and I got bounced around the most and lots of time I almost got thrown out and you and Towner just laughed." That was the first thing she remembers. And the second?

"And you and Towner could just 'go' over the side and you never wanted to paddle over to shore for me so I just had to 'hold it' all day or else paddle myself but you never helped me and everyone knows one person can't paddle a rubber raft by themselves so

I was always miserable."

I'm not admitting that those memories are accurate — just that Sandy remembers it that way. Anyway, she still thought another trip with her big brother would be fun, even if not memorable and that's why neither one of us remembers how we got to Cuzco even though we know we must have had fun.

"I've been on so many trips, how am I supposed to remember?" she asked when I pressed her for accurate details.

"I didn't expect you to remember," I admitted, "but I certainly expected you to be able to make something up and act like you remembered." I was clearly disappointed and I could see her mind working fast trying to rescue her reputation as a story teller.

Sandy was a fun traveling companion even when she couldn't remember any details. At five feet two inches and 98 pounds, she was built tough and wiry. She wasn't into nice clothes and fancy makeup, didn't have to have her dishwater blonde hair perfectly in place and didn't mind spending nights sleeping in the dirt or the back of trucks or on boulders. Since she didn't whine and complain, we could easily spend days on end having fun being miserable together. And if we couldn't remember what had actually happened, she could usually come up with a pretty good recreation that made it sound better than it was.

What we do know for sure is that we spent a couple of days in Cuzco smack in the middle of its busiest time for tourists. In fact we joined several thousand of them for the annual celebration of Inti Raymi on June 22, the southern hemisphere's winter solstice. The Incas had always performed ceremonies and sacrifices that day to make sure the sun wouldn't continue to just move further and further south until it disappeared.

On this particular day there was a pretend sacrifice of a llama, which wasn't terribly convincing because the llama kept escaping from the table of sacrifice. Oh well, the pageantry and the costumes and the music were outstanding.

After banging around government offices with no success, we left Cuzco on a train headed for Machu Picchu, site of the famous ruins of the ancient Inca city. We were really on our way to Mantaro by train, truck, canoe, trail and small plane but for starters we'd spend a few hours in Machu Picchu since it was right on the way. That night we'd hopefully catch another train to Quillabamba.

At the station in Machu Picchu we checked our bags and boarded a diesel bus for the long, switchbacked ride up to the ruins. Little did we know that although we had both been to Machu Picchu several times by then, we had missed one of its most exciting features — one that few tourists ever get to experience.

"Let's just skip the regular stuff and go up Huayna Picchu," I suggested. Sandy was in full agreement since we had long since gotten bored listening to guides explain things that no one is actually sure of.

Huayna Picchu is the tall, craggy pinnacle overlooking the whole area. It was a favorite climb of ours and took about 45 minutes because I had to keep waiting for her to catch her breath. If she were writing this book, she'd be waiting for me to catch my breath. The point is, it's hard to breathe when you're climbing straight up at 16,000 feet.

When we got to the top, we were ready for a long relaxing rest, so we spread out on the big boulders that formed the peak. Sandy, ever eager to scare herself unnecessarily, spread eagled on a massive flat boulder and sort of scootched herself out to where she could look over the edge, straight down a thousand feet to the churning muddy waters of the Urubamba River. Suddenly, I heard a gasp.

"Ronny," she half whispered in a voice that sounded like she'd just scared herself even more than she wanted to, "the rock moved." I burst out laughing.

"That rock can't move," I mocked. "It's huge and it's been up here for aeons. How's it going to move?"

"It moved," she said with conviction and bulging eyes. "I know it moved." She scootched herself backwards sort of like a lizard that's gotten stuck in tree sap and suddenly gasped again, terror all over her slithering body. "It moved again."

Well, I took her picture so I could use it to taunt her later, then spread eagled on the rock myself. I slithered out toward the edge even though I don't particularly like looking straight down a thousand feet. For some peculiar psychological reason, it makes me want to jump, which isn't all that good of an idea.

Suddenly a tremor shot through my body. The whole huge boulder tipped.

Now, if I tell you how much it tipped, you'll just laugh because half an inch isn't very impressive and you'll think we're just a couple of weenies. But let me tell you something: when you're on top of a skinny little pinnacle, stretching way out to one edge and looking down into eternity, half of an inch can make you completely loose control of your continence, which neither of us did but both of us came close to. It was one of the more frightening moments of my life and one I went back for again and again on future trips. If you ever want to experience it, I'll be glad to take you.

At 4:00 we ran all the way down to the train station, passing up the bus ride to enjoy the scenery, listen to the screeching parrots and, more importantly, save $5.00 each. The great thing about budget travel is that you get to see so much more than you want to. This hour's walk/slide down the mountain was definitely worth the effort, except that the first few steep short cuts we took were obviously bush latrines. We made a lot of split-second decisions about where to land our feet as we plunged down the steep trail.

Of course we needn't have rushed. Other trains came and went, hauling off tourists by the hundreds, and still we sat. I paced the tiny station reading signs to amuse myself and noticed that the train schedule had been helpfully divided into two sections, labeled in English: "Scheduled trains," and "Eventual Trains." Ours, of course, was an eventual train, which I didn't think was encouraging.

Our eventual train finally clattered into the station about 8:00, its horn blasting and echoing. The engineer apparently wasn't impressed by just two lonely passengers standing forlornly in front of the station.

"Hurry!" I shouted to Sandy. "He's not going to stop." The train had slowed down, but that was it. Sandy and I grabbed our duffels, which each weighed about as much as the train, dragged them frantically along the gravel beside the tracks, grunted them into the doorway as we jogged and leaped in on top of them, panting.

This definitely wasn't a tourist train. Every seat and most of the aisle was jammed with peasants and their considerable baggage, returning home from a day of buying and selling at the market in Cuzco. As the train swayed and lurched on the uneven, narrow-gauge tracks, Sandy and I crammed our stuff and ourselves into any space we could find and prepared ourselves for 21/2 hours of second-hand cigarette smoke and clattering exhaustion. No wonder she loved traveling with me.

In Quillabamba we found a ratty hotel, took cold showers down the hall and slept for a few hours in beds that were shaped sort of like hammocks and definitely didn't offer superior back support. Early in the morning we went to the market for glasses of freshly whizzed fruit juice that tasted heavenly and probably would send us there prematurely given the impurities in the water. Then we found an open-bed truck headed on down river, once again heaved our bags in and climbed aboard.

All day under a scorching sun the truck jostled us and 30 or 40 other passengers further and further into the jungle on a dirt road. Beside us the Urubamba River grew bigger and faster. We slowly worked our way through several fresh landslides where we could look straight down into the river far below, sometimes not seeing any road between the truck and the dropoff. More than once we looked straight down to where other buses and trucks hadn't made it. A heavy layer of dust turned us all from white skins and brown skins to uniformly gray skins, so that we could only tell each other apart by the color of our eyes.

When we got to the end of the road, we asked around to see if any Machis were waiting for us. We had told them by radio what our plans were and asked them to come get us in a canoe. That had been a long time ago and anything could have happened to them or us by now. In any case, no one was there.

"Does anyone have horses to help get us down to the mouth of the Kompiroshiato River?" I asked. There was at least a trail that far. Helpful people considered all the possibilities and pretty much said "no." In fact, they definitely said "no."

"Then how about porters?" I asked. "Is there anyone we could pay to carry our things?" There was no roaring enthusiasm for that idea, either. Apparently they had seen our bags. "Boats?" None in town.

"Well," said Sandy, "We can just carry our stuff." That's what I liked about Sandy — she weighed about 98 pounds and she was quite optimistic about the possibility of carrying her 200 pound bag for 10 hours over a rocky trail that climbed and dipped steeply as it followed the river. "I'm sure we can do it." Normally when she said stuff like that she crossed fingers or toes in case it didn't work out later, but I couldn't see anything crossed this time, so she must have been relatively serious.

After exhausting all of the possibilities and ourselves, we left it in God's capable hands for the night, spread our blankets on a sandbar and passed a fitful night listening to the rapids and the inevitable drunks that hang out in frontier shanty towns where there is nothing to do but sit around a table and slurp the night away.

In the morning we had a breakfast of greasy fried eggs and delicious fried bananas. We weren't in a rush to start hiking. Theoretically if we just had enough patience, some Machis would arrive within a few days and take us to Shimaa, where we could catch a plane to Mantaro.

Unfortunately Quiteni in those days wasn't an easy place to be patient. Sanitation facilities were zero, loose pigs wandered at will, men with hangovers hassled us endlessly and food services left us feeling after each meal like we'd just had an oil change. It wasn't a typical Peruvian town and by nine a.m. we'd had enough.

"Where does the trail start?" I asked a shopkeeper who had been part of the horse, porter and boat discussions.

"You mean the trail to the Kompiroshiato?" he answered with arched eyebrows. "You mean you're going to just walk by yourselves?" I guess he had never really considered the possibility that two white people would actually do it. I nodded and he pointed.

Using our belts and some rope we made tumplines for our huge bags, supported them from our foreheads, took our shoes off and started walking. Or maybe crawling would be a better word. The very first part of the trail was a steep scramble on loose shale and by the time we'd gone fifteen minutes we were drained. That's when we realized that we hadn't brought any water along, which strikes me as pretty poor planning on Sandy's part. I mean, as I remember it, she was in charge of water. As she remembers it, I was in charge of everything, but then you already know that she doesn't remember it very well.

We were thirsty. Thirsty in a dehydrated kind of way that makes you not think too clearly. There wasn't much shade along the trail, since it clung to the steep banks of the river and the sun broiled us mercilessly. Our feet were soon gashed from the pounding on sharp rocks. Our heavy bags threw us off balance repeatedly as they rocked back and forth on our backs. The humidity blanketed and suffocated us. Sweat drenched us.

I don't even remember how long we stuck it out. Four hours? Five? Six? I just know that at some point, perched high above the river desperate for some water, we gave up.

"Let's take the next trail we see down to the river," I panted. "We'll never get there this way."

The next trail down to the river ended in the front yard of a Quechua family living in an adobe hut with a thatched roof. They had apparently moved down from the mountains in search of land. We lurched straight through their yard, tumbled down a short bank, jettisoned our bags, stripped to our underwear and waded into the Urubamba. We couldn't drink it, of course, but we could at least wallow in it for a while. Heaven on scorched earth. No wonder some people worship rivers.

"Let's boil some water," I finally suggested. We dug out an old pot, built a quick fire and soon were gulping cup after cup of scalding water. We could actually feel our cells swelling with relief.

Although we were pretty grateful we

weren't dead, we were somewhat disheartened about being stuck, with no clue of when or how we would go on. It could be an hour or a week, and even though we'd rather be stuck on a clean sandbar in the middle of the jungle than in Quiteni, we still needed to get to Mantaro sooner or later. The Quechua family was sympathetic and fascinated, but they didn't have a boat.

We slept under the stars and woke up soaked with dew, covered with wet sand. Our gracious neighbors invited us to come for breakfast, so we followed our stocky hostess' long black braids, embroidered blouse and layers of skirts into a tiny dining area with a tinier table and two benches. She waited until we were seated by ourselves, then headed for the kitchen where coffee was obviously percolating. The only light came from a small opening over my head. Animals on the other side of the wall grunted and bleated.

Breakfast was a feast: generous portions of boiled chicken, boiled manioc and boiled bananas. The only problem was the coffee, which was so thick and black you could have paved a road with it. Both Sandy and I love the smell of coffee, but the actual stuff gives us upset stomachs and vibrating nerves even when it's weak. This particular batch would have had us swinging from the rafters and chattering like monkeys. On the other hand, it would be rude not to drink it. I took a quick look around to make sure the lady wasn't coming, grabbed my coffee cup and whipped it up over my head in one clean motion, tossing the contents through the window into the pen. A pig squealed, but at least I didn't hear any people yelping.

"Quick, do mine too," whispered Sandy urgently. I traded her cups, made it two clean shots in a row and when the lady came back we looked politely grateful, with clean plates and empty cups.

"Mas caf?" she asked. We said no thank you, we'd had plenty. She's probably still wondering how we ever forced down the thick sludge that always settles to the bottom of a cup of mountain coffee.

We thanked our hostess with genuine gratitude, then walked back down to our little beach and went for a swim. Read our books, went for another swim, read our books some more. With no radio to find out what was going on, no boat and no desire to walk back the way we'd come, all we could do was wait for help. It could be a very long wait.

Chapter 13

The Mantaro Trail

In the last chapter, I left you
waiting with Sandy and me on a
sandbar. It's a shame you get to go
on to this chapter so quickly. You
should have to wait much longer to
find out what happened.

Fortunately we didn't wait long
ourselves. Around midmorning, we
saw a slender dugout canoe coming
slowly upriver, two slim but
powerful Machi men poling against
the strong current. When they

finally got close enough I gave the appropriate greeting ("You?") and they gave the appropriate answer ("Me.") and I asked where they had come from ("Shimaa").

"Where are you going?" I continued with rising hope.

"We're coming to get you," they answered. If they were surprised to find us on a little sandbar a long way from Quiteni, they didn't show it. "The teacher sent us."

Why had I ever doubted? In spite of the logistical hassles, the Machis would always do their best to take care of us. It would cost them two full days just to pick us up and they would have waited patiently for us in Quiteni for several days if necessary. They carefully loaded our bags in the canoe, told us where to sit, turned the canoe around and never even asked how we had gotten there.

After a short drift down the Urubamba and a long haul up the Kompiroshiato, pulling the canoe through shallow rapids until dark, we ended up in Shimaa for the night. The next day a small airplane from Yarinacocha collected us and whizzed us to Mantaro — a picture perfect flight over fiercely rugged mountains. As I looked down on steep cliffs and tangled trees, I tried to imagine hiking the same route overland and didn't relish the thought. But that's exactly what I was about to do.

Mantaro, with about a hundred people, was the most isolated of all the Machi villages. Venturo, the pioneer school teacher who formed the village, had braved raging rivers and treacherous trails to visit Machis who lived scattered in remote valleys, along small streams. With his encouragement, many had moved into the village so they could take advantage of the school and medical help. They were extremely hospitable, unusually energetic, and terribly eager to develop their community. But they couldn't.

The main source of income for the Machis came from selling produce like coffee, beans, rice, chocolate, peanuts and animal skins to outsiders. It was about the only way they had to get money for the manufactured goods they badly wanted, including cloth, fishhooks, machetes, medicines, cooking pots and other things that we take for granted.

There weren't many large mammals in Mantaro, so hide sales were out. On the other hand, Mantaro was a perfect place for growing coffee and chocolate if only they could find a way to get their produce out to market. The unpredictable river beside their village was only navigable part of the time and then only with precarious balsa rafts. It was too expensive to fly produce out on small airplanes. What they needed was an overland route to the nearest good river, and Dad wanted me to encourage them to find one.

When Sandy and I arrived, we were swallowed up in friendliness and papayas. Actually I guess we swallowed up the papayas, which grew all over the village. The people of Mantaro were extremely responsive to suggestions about how to improve their lives, so when someone said fruit would be good for them they planted enough papayas to feed the whole tribe.

We were given one papaya that weighed 11 pounds and ate it all by ourselves. Can you imagine? Newborn babies don't even weigh 11 pounds. And the good thing about newborn babies is that they don't give you diarrhea, which papayas do and is something I should have thought more about.

"So where do you think we should try to go with the trail?" I asked Venturo over a dinner of fish and manioc and papaya. Venturo was a frail, serious man. All of his considerable stamina came from the inside and from the support of his tiny, dimpled wife.

"Shimaa would be the closest," he said. "If they can get to Shimaa, they can take their stuff down the river to the road."

"Is there anyone who would go with me to check it out?" I asked.

"No," he said. Which didn't exactly mean "no," but it would take a while to find out what it did mean. We went on to other topics and during a pause he asked, "How many men would you need?"

"I don't know. Maybe five or six so they could help cut the trail and see for themselves what it's like."

"Well," he said, "I'll go with you."

We talked of other things, caught up on the news and periodically came back to the trail exploration.

"How many more would you need?" he asked.

"Maybe four or five," I suggested.

"I think my brother would go with us."

And so it went into the evening, patiently putting together a team by playing stereotypic Machi mind games. A Machi would never just say that he had something you asked for, nor would he ever immediately announce that he had a whole crew of people standing by eager to help. After all, if the quantity he had in mind wasn't what you had in mind, then you might be disappointed and think less of him.

Whether it was bushels of peanuts or stalks of bananas or people for a project, if you asked for it, they didn't have it. Then, slowly but surely they would get a feel for what you expected and rise to meet it, never letting you think they had as much as you might want until they were sure that was *all* you really wanted.

In the morning we had a party of six men. They came to Sandy's and my hut dressed in red paint and cushmas, each carrying a machete, a small bag and a wad of coca leaves in his cheek. The leaves would keep them from getting tired, hungry or thirsty on the trail and I wished for some myself.

As we walked away from the hut, leaving Sandy in the care of the village people for a week, I had a sick feeling in my guts. It didn't have anything to do with leaving Sandy, who would be safer there than in any city in the U.S. The pain was more specific than that — the familiar feeling of amoebic dysentery and too much papaya.

I belched sulphuric fumes and my bowels cramped mercilessly and all my enthusiastic anticipation of an exciting hike through the jungle evaporated, leaving "miserable" as the only possible adjective. I was paying for the whizzy fruit drink that had been so delicious and malicious.

We started off down our side of the river, then waded across and headed into the jungle, climbing steeply. Within half an hour I had dropped back to squat behind a tree, then again within another twenty minutes, then again within the hour. When I stood back up, my head spun dizzily and I reached for some Entero Vioformo, which has since been banned because of its side effects. Right then I welcomed any side effects that promised to kill me quickly.

I hadn't planned well, counting on the Machis to bring everything we needed except my clothes and blanket. I figured they'd bring food, so I didn't. I had a small water bottle, but it was empty in an hour and I had no water purification tablets. As my energy drained out of me, rather literally, I struggled to act like everything was fine. I didn't, after all, want them to turn back on my account.

We had no good trail to follow, but the Machis had an unerring instinct for which way to go and took advantage of faint animal paths along the way. If I hadn't been so preoccupied with just moving my legs and breathing, I would have exulted in the beauty of the rugged jungle, the bird calls, the overwhelming greenery. But all of that was a little hard with me feeling my own overwhelming shade of green.

The whole first day we climbed and I tried to picture men carrying 100-pound bags of coffee beans along this route. It didn't seem possible, even though Machi men perform stunning feats of strength and endurance every day of their lives. Strangely enough, we crossed no streams the whole first day. We scavenged what water we could out of leaves and once in a while cut open stalks of bamboo to drain out a few swallows.

Venturo and I looked tired, but the others forged ahead strongly, chewing their power leaves and making blaze marks on tree trunks. We had no snack breaks and no lunch, except that once in a while when we passed the right kind of palm tree we'd rip out the heart and get a bite or two of pulp. I would happily have traded 250 bites of the stuff for one good bologna sandwich.

We camped right in the jungle, high on the side of a mountain under a shelter of leaves. I was famished and happily swallowed my small share of boiled manioc. Better than nothing. The trots were easing up a bit, presumably because there wasn't anything left in the whole lower half of my body. By flashlight we checked ourselves for wood ticks and then fell asleep on the ground. Only a couple of us had blankets; the rest just tucked their arms and legs and heads into their robes.

Ironically, different parts of me kept falling asleep during the night, keeping the rest of me awake. First a leg, then an arm, then a foot, then the other arm. It was rather annoying to keep waking up because bits were falling asleep.

It was pitch dark, without a shred of light under the jungle canopy. If we hadn't had flashlights, we would have been blind men until morning. Tiny feet scampered noisily through the leaves. Dew dripped from high above us. Tree frogs boinked, bonked and beeped, some sounding just like car alarms going off. Insects shrilled. A whole different set of animals took over the jungle when the sun went down.

The second day was worse than the first. We left at daylight and immediately began working our way up, over and down steep ridges covered with vegetation. At times we perched precariously on tree roots that clung tightly to rock faces. If we weren't careful, someone would step onto what looked like a secure footing, only to fall through a layer of moss that stretched from root to root. At one point, we stopped to rest on such a narrow ridge that we had to sit single file along its length. It didn't take much of an I.Q. to understand why this wasn't a world class trade route.

Early in the afternoon we came to a sheer drop. Without hesitating for a moment, the men whacked down tall saplings and lashed them together into a long ladder, notching the rails so that the cross pieces would hold firmly. It was an unforgettable privilege to watch them work, quickly and skillfully crafting a route down the cliff.

One man particularly caught my eye. He was a little older than the rest, tall and wild looking with high cheekbones, tangled hair, tattoos on his face and a big smile. He never said much the whole time and had struck me as a little self-conscious, but he did more than his share of the work. But now I noticed that he was having a little trouble negotiating the long, shaky ladder.

I watched curiously as my "brother" gathered up his robe, tucked his machete under his arm and carefully worked his way down. He was only using one hand and I began to wonder if he had hurt the other one.

"What's wrong with his other arm?" I asked Venturo privately. Venturo looked at me blankly, as if I had just asked a stupid question.

"He doesn't have another one," he said. "He was born with just one."

We had been climbing and traversing and cutting in some of the most rugged terrain I'd ever been in, and I'd never noticed. I was stunned.

"How does he clear his fields and hunt?" I asked. It would be impossible to use a bow and arrow or an axe with just one arm.

"He fishes with a spear and clears with a machete. He can do almost anything, including playing the flute." I was humbled to realize that he could do far more than I could with two good arms and hands. "These people are amazing," Venturo continued with genuine admiration. He apparently didn't know that I thought he was amazing too.

When we were all down the ladder we headed more or less on down into a new watershed. As darkness fell, we were once again tucked into a little leaf shelter eating a few mouthfuls of manioc, our stomachs growling and my energy down to zero. The conversation pretty much centered around how this wouldn't work as a way to get produce out to market. It was obvious to everyone that carrying bags down ladders wasn't exactly optimal and would probably kill everyone before it made them any money. Still, we would go on down to Shimaa. It would be a nice opportunity to visit long lost relatives and catch up on news.

The third day we had a lucky break. As we broke out onto a huge gravel bar beside the Shimaa River around mid day, we came across a lone Machiguenga sitting beside a crackling campfire. He had built a rack over the fire so he could smoke various monkeys that he'd shot during that morning and their whole bodies lay stretched out, black and tough. They looked delicious.

Well, we weren't *that* lucky. He didn't particularly want to share the best part of his catch with so many of us, but he did have their guts in a pan sitting directly on the flame, looking like a mess of huge white noodles. I can't say they looked delicious, but after being sick for three days and not eating much, I wasn't about to be picky. When he offered me a spoon and pointed to the pot, I greedily plunged in and slurped long strings of intestines that hadn't been cleaned very well. Apparently that was usually his wife's job. A little salt would sure help, I thought, but didn't let it stop me.

My stomach flip flopped, but since I wasn't quite throwing up I just kept going and he was very gratified at how much I liked his soup. It was somehow reassuring that I was already sick, so this couldn't make me feel much worse. A little salt would have really helped.

We visited for a while, then continued on down the river enjoying the relatively easy walk along beaches and banks. Late in the afternoon we arrived in Shimaa and were welcomed with real food, real houses and a real place to bathe. I thought I'd died and gone to heaven.

My old friend Pedro was the teacher and his wife made sure that I wouldn't get hungry during the night. He and Venturo had known each other for many years when they went to school together, so they talked long into the night. Long after I'd fallen asleep on a woven reed mat under a cozy mosquito net.

"We'll go home another way," Venturo

told me in the morning. "The way we came was impossible." I considered telling him I'd rather just stay here the rest of my life, which felt like it was about over anyway, than walk back to Mantaro. But I couldn't, of course, because I was there to encourage them. Or whatever.

Without so much as a day's rest we went on down the Shimaa to where it met the Kompiroshiato River and headed upstream. By following it up to a crossover, we could once again climb high over another pass and drop into the headwaters of the Mantaro River valley. I won't kill you with the details. There's no way to make them funny.

By the time we had spent the whole third day crisscrossing the Mantaro River I was soaked to the bone, looked like a prune and couldn't keep my pants from falling down. The Machis, of course, looked like they'd just walked across the street for some soda pop. I plopped down on the porch while Sandy stared at what was left of me. Just for chuckles, we got out a spring scale and found that I'd lost 15 pounds. There are a lot of Americans who would pay good money for a trip like that.

"Well?" asked Sandy. "Did you find a trail?"

"No." We bought a chicken, chased it until we could finally grab it, butchered it and dug into another papaya while the chicken boiled. I slept that night like a man in a coma.

The next day we received word by radio that a plane was coming to pick us up and would we please bring in 50 kilos of peanuts?

"Do any of you have peanuts you want to sell?" I asked the people sitting on our porch:

"No," they all answered. Which didn't exactly mean 'no', of course. I forgot all about it while we packed our stuff.

"How many peanuts do you need?" a beautiful young woman asked.

"About 50 kilos," I answered.

"Oh. Well, I only have five," she offered hopefully. I smiled a very grateful smile.

Three hours later we left Mantaro with over 50 kilos of peanuts.

"Could you fly over to Shimaa on our way out?" I asked the pilot. "I want to see where we went."

"Sure," he said. Three minutes later we were over Shimaa, waving our wings at the people below. It had taken a little longer, the pilot said, because we had to gain enough altitude to fly over the pass. "Oh," I said.

Within a few years the whole village of Mantaro had moved to a different river so they could sell their coffee. My brother still clears the jungle, spears fish and plays the flute with one arm.

Chapter 14

Death Of The Rubber Raft

The summer of 1972 was running out. Sandy and I got back to Yarinacocha with just a few weeks left until we'd both have to head to the U.S. That gave us just enough time to plan a final group campout to the Boqueron. We invited all of the summer guest helpers and local high schoolers and even a few of the more adventurous adults living on the center.

Every summer groups of guest

helpers including high school students, college students and even some adults came to Yarinacocha to help out. Sometimes they had relatives on the center, or they were from churches that supported a linguist, or they'd just heard about us and wanted to have a part. Whatever, we and the chiggers loved them.

We loved them because they were a welcome source of help during the summer months when help was short. Many of the regular personnel were gone on furloughs to their home countries, so the temporary personnel ran children's summer programs, did basic repair and maintenance on homes and buildings, built airstrips in remote areas, and lent hands where they were needed most. They were pretty naïve and gullible, which made them a lot more fun.

The chiggers loved them because chiggers love soft new skin. They'd make furiously itchy welts in the most inconvenient places to scratch and it was pretty funny sometimes to watch people scratch when they were trying not to let anyone know they were. You could always tell who the newcomers were by their welts and their intricate scratch dances.

I always got a special kind of pleasure in helping the short termers have a good time. I mean, a good time by our standards, which I'm not too sure was the same thing as a good time by their standards.

In those days, no summer at Yarinacocha would have been complete without a campout to the Boqueron, where you kind of had to stretch your definition of "good time" to include nights sleeping in the rain and days stuck between landslides. It was at least a chance to get out of the lowland heat and stare at waterfalls, blue morpho butterflies, raging white water and high cliffs covered with ferns.

I was particularly looking forward to this Boqueron trip. It would be my last one, as far as I could tell, for a long time. Besides, I had my rubber raft parked in the shed out behind our house. It seemed to me that the raft would be an ideal way to run the river that snarled its way through the narrow gorge and I hadn't heard of anyone having done it before. If you've read all three of my books, you surely understand by now that I at least had to try it.

Back then there weren't all that many people in Peru who even had rubber rafts. I was lucky to have brought mine down from the U.S. with me, but of course I didn't bring a very good one because those cost too much and weigh way too much. For some reason I thought if you could do something in a multi-thousand dollar 10-man neoprene raft with an experienced guide and all the best helmets and paddles, then you could do it just as well in a $200 6-man vinyl raft with no experience and plastic oars.

My family rented the center's stake bed truck for our trip. It was a mid-sized truck with a mid-sized bed that was surrounded by a wooden fence kind of thing. It had a suspension that would rattle fillings out of teeth and had no cover in case of rain.

Getting a large group together was quite easy.

"Do you want to go camping at the Boqueron with my family?" I'd ask.

"Sure," they'd say until they'd had enough experience to automatically say no to anything I suggested. "What do I need to bring?"

"Oh, not much. We'll throw in some food for everyone, so just make sure you've got your bedding and something to swim in." We always went pretty basic because there wasn't a lot of space and besides, we knew everything we took would come back wet, muddy and smelly.

"What kind of bedding?" Well, as you can imagine, I wasn't ever very helpful there. We'd spent so many nights miserable that it didn't seem fair not to let our guests have the same wonderful memories to look back on. So...

"Oh, just a blanket and a piece of plastic to put under yourself." I might have added that it would probably rain, but that never seemed all that relevant in the planning stage, and I certainly didn't want to discourage anyone from going. No one had tents anyway, so there was no point in telling everyone that they'd probably need one.

We jammed 20 or so of us and our gear into the back of the truck where we could sit and stand on each other for about five hours. If you want to know what the drive out was like, read my first two books. If you want to know why we thought a trip like that was fun, well … let's just say you had to be there. Faces full of dust, kidneys knocked completely loose from their attachments, sun broiling our brains, three or four songs going at once, all sung badly and loudly.

Late in the afternoon we dumped our skimpy sleeping gear on the ground, cooked a supper under threatening skies and sang ourselves to sleep by the roaring river. We knew that by morning we would all be soaked, but that never discouraged us, nor did it ever motivate us to put up shelters. Spending the night in soggy blankets was part of the Boqueron experience and if anyone actually got a good night's sleep, they'd feel like they'd been cheated.

In the morning after breakfast I walked along the road upriver a ways to see where we might launch the raft. I remember thinking that the river looked a little wild for such a small raft, but I also thought that my apprehension was only due to my lack of experience. Surely once we were on the water we would see that "these rafts could go through anything," as I had been saying over and over while recruiting passengers.

I am now older and wiser. Nothing that I'm about to say should encourage anyone to do something so stupid. It was a different world, where we didn't even think about life jackets and helmets and good paddles. We just plunged in and kids just like us have died because of it. But this is all looking back. At the time, it seemed reasonably sensible, except to Mom, who probably just bit her lip and hummed gospel choruses, which she tended to do when things got a bit nerve wracking.

That's not to say I wasn't a bit scared and it seemed a good idea to try out the raft on a short stretch of the river first. We took turns pumping it up with a foot action pump until it was tight as a balloon. Then we carried it a couple hundred yards upriver, gingerly climbed our way down the steep rocky bank and set it in the water. I climbed in with a couple other guys and we floated through a relatively mild section, experimenting with the paddles and finding that we had a moderately good degree of control.

The raft bounced high on the waves and

we waved to family and friends who watched from the high bank. Big smiles, huge boost in confidence, no problem. If we could do so well with two people in a calm section, surely we could do it with twice as many people in a rough section, I thought. Maybe I'd been in the sun too long the day before.

It wasn't hard to get passengers, I'm sorry to say. Everyone wanted to be in on the thrill of being first. I ended up with Jeff Elder, Mark Friesen, Dee What's Her Name who was one of the summer helpers and myself. Jeff had paddled a canoe on a lake, Mark had grown up on rivers similar to the ones where I grew up and Dee wanted to find out what it was like to be in a boat.

Since we only had two paddles, I didn't think it mattered much that two of my passengers hadn't had a lot of river experience. All they had to do was hang on for dear life at the appropriate times. Dee, I was sure, would think it appropriate to hang on for dear life the whole way.

Once again we headed up the muddy road, but farther this time. I wanted to get upriver from some good turbulence to have the best time possible, so had picked a spot just up from a little waterfall. As I said above, it's worth repeating that we didn't have any life jackets, didn't have any helmets, didn't have any sense.

We slowly slid the raft down the rocks and carefully scrambled down after it, trying to keep from puncturing it on sharp edges. It was a long way down, all wet from the rain. About halfway Jeff lost his footing and fell hard on his right arm.

"Are you okay?" I shouted above the roar of the river. "Did you break anything?"

"Yes" to the first question and "no" to the second, he answered through clenched teeth. "But I can't move my arm."

"Do you still want to try it?" I asked.

"Oh yeah, I'll be all right." He didn't even hesitate, probably thinking that he could still hang on for dear life with one arm and in any case it would be easier than trying to scramble back up the bank.

We got to the bottom of the bank and set the raft into a backwater so it wouldn't race off without us. Jeff got in first, front left, Dee second, front right, Mark third, back right with a paddle and me last, back left with a paddle. Without giving instructions or offering prayers, I pushed us off.

I might as well acknowledge that anyone with even a few hours of rafting experience knows that there are technical terms for everything a river does. I even know some of them, but it doesn't make a whole lot of difference right now and it didn't then. It's enough to know that rivers boil and swirl and burble and swallow and tumble and crash and get so mixed up that sometimes you don't know if the current is going forward or backward or both. That's why they're so fun to swim in, not that we wanted to swim in this particular one.

There's nothing like the exhilaration of discovering that you're in over your head, which we did within seconds. We immediately rushed for a narrow opening between two big boulders, where the current dropped off about six feet. Mark and I paddled furiously as if we knew what we were doing, but when we hit the drop, the sudden lurch smashed the right side of the raft into one of the boulders and broke Mark's paddle.

"Wow," we gasped collectively when we'd gotten back into our positions. "That was cool! This thing is amazing!" At least we hoped so.

Fortunately the raft only filled a quarter full of water on our way through. I was getting more scared by the minute, since rubber rafts pretty much just spin in circles if you only have one paddle and a raft that's filling with water weighs tons. That wasn't a happy thought, even if we were trying to get as much adventure out of the trip as possible. Like my Machiguenga friends, I hid my fears with jokes and bravado.

Besides, there was no stopping now. We whooshed along toward a spot where the full current smashed into a rocky cliff and breathed big sighs of relief when we bounced off still right side up. A short break from the rapids gave us time to worry about the steel reinforcing bars sticking out of pieces of an old bridge, but there wasn't much I could do about it and we didn't have to worry long. We missed them by inches. The best was yet to come.

Right in front of where everyone would be watching, we headed straight for a wildly cascading dropoff, no thanks to me. This was the heart of our run, our moment of glory, our last chance to wonder if there was anything in our lives to repent of. The wind blew our hair as we picked up speed and dove right over the edge in a tumultuous roar. Stopped dead. Stuck.

When water pours over a rock and falls a couple of feet or more it creates a backwater on the downriver side that sucks things right up against the rock. It's a fun place to river surf if you know what you're doing, but we didn't and it wasn't a fun place to be stuck. Water gushed into the raft, the waves bounced us mercilessly and I couldn't get us out. None of the others looked as if they thought they were having fun.

In fact, leaning over the edge to get as much leverage on my paddle as I could, I suddenly got bounced right out of the raft and pulled under. Banged against a few rocks, turned head over heels without knowing which was up and was about to decide it was time to panic when I surfaced as suddenly as I had gone under.

When I came up gasping for air I was 50 yards down from the raft and my back was scraped and by the time I used my fingernails to drag myself onto a boulder in the middle of the river I knew I was lucky. I wasn't so sure about the three people left in the raft without any paddle. They looked as if they were seeing scenes from the afterlife.

Somehow during my swim the raft had broken free of the backwater. It was headed pretty close to where I stood on my boulder and our last chance to get it stopped was to pull it onto my perch.

"Give me your hand," I ordered Jeff, who was still front left. When he got close enough we reached for each other's good arms, locked wrists with viselike grips and I pulled as if their lives depended on it. Pulled so hard, in fact, that I pulled Jeff right out of the raft onto the rock. He and I perched there, panting, while Mark and Dee sped off still wildly out of control, into heavier water and maybe watery heaven.

"Hang on," I shouted to them. Not that weren't already.

There's no way to tell this as fast as it happened. There I was on a boulder in the middle of the roaring river with Jeff who couldn't swim because he had one bad arm and Mark and Dee rushing off in a raft full of water with no way to steer or control it and all I could think was that I had to get downstream from them and try to intercept them and people were high on the bank above us with their mouths hanging open and not able to help because they couldn't get down to the river so I leaped into the water and swam toward shore and made it just before I went through another wild rapid and crawled out with my heart pounding and raced hopping and slipping from rock to rock along the shore trying to catch up with the raft which was of course going faster than I could except that for a few merciful seconds it got caught in another backwater and I lunged and grabbed and held onto it and finally got it stopped and now Dee really didn't look like she was having very much fun but she was certainly hanging on!

Take a breath. Take several.

"Are you okay?" I asked. I think maybe I should feel guilty about the fact that that's the question I've had to ask most when I invite people to do something with me.

Dee didn't answer and I wondered briefly if she'd lost her voice along with all the blood in her face. I'm not sure why she wasn't jumping up and down wild with joy at being alive, at knowing what it was like to go rafting through the Boqueron, at the sheer ecstasy of knowing that she had a great story to tell for the rest of her life. Instead she just sort of sat there in a daze, absent-mindedly scratching chigger welts.

We eventually got everyone out of the raft and dumped the water out of it, which wasn't hard because the bottom was full of huge holes. Then we worked our way back upriver to collect Jeff and all regrouped at our campsite. We checked everyone for injuries and found that my back and Jeff's elbow were about all that mattered.

I had a patch kit for the raft, but it wasn't exactly designed to replace the whole bottom. Besides, without paddles no one wanted to retrace our exhilarating route, which shows that we were smarter than you thought there for a while. We relaxed, enjoyed life, thought someday this would all be funny. Happily threw away the raft.

You would have thought that would be the end of it, but actually it was only the end of the raft. There was still this little mystery about the whole experience because none of us knew where the river, that we'd sort of run went after it left the Boqueron. I thought the least we could do, having failed at one thing, would be to find out.

Ron Barkey, whose name repeatedly comes up in stories that have to do with poor judgment, said he'd like to join me. This in spite of the fact that he was a school teacher and supposedly a role model exemplifying wisdom as a goal. His handicap was that he was like a part of our family, which pretty much robbed him of any inherited common sense.

Since the rubber raft was gone and there were clearly a number of pretty good stretches of white water downriver, we picked up some truck tire tubes and set off on a clear morning. We had no idea how long it would take for us to get to someplace recognizable, and since we suspected that it could be anywhere from four hours to four days, we took along some snacks and water bottles and told everyone not to worry if we didn't show up for supper.

I would happily tell you about the trip, but since we didn't break anything, didn't puncture the tubes, didn't even take more than six hours to get to the only road in the area, it just isn't interesting. The river settled down considerably once it left the Boqueron's narrow canyon and about the only great thing I can say about the trip is that it paved the way and opened up a new avenue of entertainment for future generations, who happily floated in our wakes.

No one, as far as I know, has yet run the Boqueron in a rubber raft, in case you want to be famous.

In the meantime, the translation of the New Testament inched steadily forward, one word at a time. Twenty-two years, and the Machis still waited.

Chapter 15

The Dedication

During the six-year span of this book, the Scripture translation work slowly crept along verse by tedious verse. At times it seemed to grind almost to a frustrating halt while Dad and Mom searched for exactly the right way to translate a word or a phrase, cared for critically ill Machis, or rescued their own kids from badly planned adventures.

A good translator has to be a creative detective, constantly looking for new ways to solve mysteries. The goal of the Machi translation was to provide them with Scriptures that had the very same information and emotional impact as it did in the original languages. That was no easy task, especially given the cultural differences between the Machiguengas and the Hebrews, Greeks and Romans.

Lush rainforest instead of sandy desert. Tapirs, monkeys and jaguars instead of sheep, goats and camels. Hunting and gathering instead of sheepherding and wheat fields. Manioc, bananas and sweet potatoes instead of bread, grapes and olives. Head men of tiny family groups instead of kings, governors and tax collectors.

For the Machis, being stingy was the worst sin and getting angry was pretty much in the same category. On the other hand, being a good hunter was the ultimate high quality of a man and the one he would present to the father of the girl he wanted to marry. That wasn't something the Apostle Paul ever wrote much about.

Every chapter presented a new set of problems. For example, in April of 1973 my parents were in the middle of the last major revision of the New Testament. After years of searching they still hadn't found a really good way to say, "to know God."

It wouldn't seem to be that hard: God is a person, so if a Machi could say "I know

Mario," then he should also be able to say, "I know God." Unfortunately, the Machi words for knowing a person literally mean "to see" the person. Since no one has seen God, that doesn't work.

There's another verb that means "to know," and it can be used with people, but "to know one's father" really means to treat him with the respect due to a father. That doesn't quite work either.

How about "to know what he's like?" Well, knowing what someone is like isn't the same as knowing him. Scrap that idea.

A similarly tough problem came up in I Corinthians 12: "The body is a unit, though it is made up of many parts; and though all its parts are many, they form one body. So it is with Christ. For we were all baptized by one Spirit into one body. Now the body is not made up of one part but of many."

Detectives have been known to solve murders without a body, but translating that chapter without one was nearly impossible. No matter what version of the Bible you look in, you'll find the word "body" at least a dozen times. But you won't find it even once in the Machiguenga Bible. They have no word for "body."

There was the word *"itinko,"* which was sort of like a person's trunk, but it doesn't include enough body parts. In fact, the Machis don't think of "body parts." A person has hands, feet, eyes, a nose and other bits and pieces, but not anything that could be lumped into a category of "body parts." If that's hard for you to understand, well, I don't understand it either, but they do. What they don't understand is "body."

How about a word for desert? For several years the search was on for a way to describe a desert. "The place where there is nothing?" No, there are people and plants and animals in deserts. "The place that is silent?" No, camels bawl and donkeys bray in the desert.

Nothing seemed to work and it didn't even help to take one of the brightest Machi translators to see the desert in Arizona and Nevada. Finally a quiet Machiguenga who had never been out of the jungle hesitantly suggested a word that means "a place where the atmosphere clears on arrival," or in other words, "where it never rains."

Just to double check, Dad and Mom tried that word out on one of the few Machis who was completely bilingual in Spanish and Machiguenga. When he heard the word in Machi, he immediately said, "That would mean *'desierto,'* wouldn't it?"

And so it went, year after year. 5% done, then 10%, then 50%, then 100% in rough draft. Then back over it all again and again to check for consistency, accuracy and understandability. Write it all down by hand. Type it all with smudgy black carbon copies. Leave copies behind in the village in case the plane crashes on the way to Yarina. Check for understandability. Revise it. Retype it. Recheck it. Cut and paste with real scissors and real glue, real scotch tape or real staples. Get the bugs out — meaning termites, roaches or crickets. Retype it.

When the manuscript was finally finished and ready for printing, SIL's status in Peru was precarious. Government officials had told our administration that SIL would have to leave the country at the end of 1976, abandoning incomplete projects all over the jungle and mountains.

The plan had been to have the finished product printed outside of the country where finer paper was available, but because of the political uncertainties it was decided that the Machi New Testament should be printed in Peru. That way there wouldn't be any risk of not being able to import it into the country when it was finished. It would be heavier and bulkier, but at least it would be there.

Before the year ended, the government reconsidered its decision to have SIL leave. Dad and Mom scheduled a dedication for January, 1977, providing they were still in Peru. They invited special friends and supporters from the U.S. to come and see the payoff on their investment over the years and worked together with the Machi church leadership to plan the event. There would be a service at Yarinacocha first, followed by a great celebration at Huallana in the heart of the Machiguenga area. Machis would come from every village.

Bu then delay after delay held up the printing. To start with, the whole manuscript was misplaced after it was hand carried to Lima, so Dad and a co-worker had to go in and track it down in Lima. The date of the dedication crept closer and closer. When we got word from the government that SIL's work could go on, we had a dozen guests coming down from the USA and still no Scriptures to dedicate.

In fact, the day before the dedication our guests were at Yarinacocha taking tours, scratching chigger bites and sweating like water sprinklers in the tropical humidity while we tried to find out where the Bibles were. Dad was on the radio with Lima several times that day.

"They left here four days ago on a truck," the radio operator in Lima finally told him. "It was Moises' truck — the guy who does the regular runs for us."

Well, four days was plenty of time for Moises to have driven from Lima to Pucallpa, so where was he? A quick drive around Pucallpa and a few conversations with truck drivers confirmed our worst fears: Moises was stuck behind a landslide on the other side of the Boqueron. January, the heart of the rainy season, was the worst time possible to be driving through that section, where road construction had scraped whole mountainsides bare and there were no plants to hold the soil together.

"Well, we'll just have to go after them," Dad decided late that night. "If we can get close to the landslide, we can carry some boxes across and we'll at least have a few for the ceremonies."

Two colleagues jumped into our VW bug and headed for the Boqueron, five hours away if the road was good. As the rest of us prayed and then went to bed, they approached the slide area and one of them suddenly recognized Moises' truck. He had just slopped his way through the mud, slipping and spinning and had pulled over to the side for some sleep. They woke him up and one rode with him to keep him awake through the rest of the night. The Bibles were at Yarinacocha in the morning and went directly from the truck to a small airplane headed for Huallana.

Two days later I sat under a thatched shelter with an overflow crowd of Machiguengas and guests. The village had been spit and polished, so to speak, in preparation. The church was far too small for the crowd, so a large temporary extension had been added on, made of poles and palm leaves. A stream near the village had been diverted so that it would run through a trough over a six-foot drop off, making a convenient shower for the gringos, al fresco.

Our gracious Machi hosts had even made a special outhouse for the occasion. Some of them had been to the outside world enough to know that where we come from, there is usually one bathroom for the men and another for the women. Trying to accomodate us in every way possible, they had made the same sort of facilities for us.

Right across the airstrip from the meeting room we could see the brand new outhouse. On the left side there was an entrance marked "women." On the right side, a different entrance was marked "men." The roof was low, so that we had to kind of stoop to get inside, and when we did we saw two separate holes, freshly dug. The only thing they had forgotten was the wall between them.

That night I sat on my section of a tree trunk bench, overwhelmed. It had been four years since I had been in Huallana with Jerry Hamill, but little had changed except that this time the river was chocolate brown from the heavy rains.

The night air was seasoned with campfire smoke mixed with exhaust fumes from a little gasoline generator brought in

for the occasion. In the dim light of a single
bulb I could see the faces of my friends,
Machiguengas who baby-sat me 25 years
before, Americans who had supported us
since before I was born and my Dad and
Mom, who had spent most of their married
life translating the New Testament.

The service, as planned by the
Machiguenga church leadership, ran
smoothly. Already there had been prayers,
introductions of guests and a few
testimonies. A slide show, the first ever for
the Machis, would soon give them chances
to laugh uncontrollably at ancient pictures
of themselves, their houses, their wildlife
and their gardens.

The next day there would be more
speeches and some testimonies from people
who had moved from fear to faith in the last
generation. At least that's how they would
describe it. They planned to share some of their
traditions: dancing, free-form singing, flute
playing, spinning and weaving. A banquet
would leave us all impressed by Machiguenga
hospitality, although some of the guests would
be a little hesitant at the prospect of monkey
and tapir meat, boiled bananas and manioc.
But that would be the next day.

At the moment Jose was giving a long
speech and my mind wandered across years
and faces.

Just downriver from where we sat we

could see where Dionisio, one of Dad's most promising translation helpers, drowned when the canoe he and Dad were in hit a tree and flipped. He couldn't be there to see the fruit of his brilliant contribution, but then he had already been translated himself and didn't need it.

Pedro hunched on my left. I had spent several weeks with him building an airstrip in Kompiroshiato when I was thirteen. Pedro had nearly died riding a raft in search of isolated Machiguengas. He went where we couldn't go, gave up the personal comforts of his home village for the struggles of a new village and then lost his son to poisoning by antagonistic neighbors.

On another hard wooden bench Venturo was listening intently to Jose. I had spent a week with Venturo trying to find a trail so the Machis in Mantaro could sell their produce to the outside world. Cold, hungry, thirsty, climbing improvised ladders up and down sheer cliffs, we never found a good trail. Venturo ended up leading more of his people to Jesus Christ than any other Machiguenga. He had spent hundreds of hours checking the New Testament for accuracy and had come to Huallana to collect part of the return on his investment.

Short, chubby Irene had been Mom's co-translator many times. She was almost perfectly bilingual in Spanish and Machi and probably a genuine genius, though she had never been tested. Her creativity, sense of humor and commitment to the translation work never ceased to amaze Mom. Dad often told them, tongue in cheek, to quit giggling and take their work more seriously.

Irene was endlessly amazed and amused by the antics of the Pharisees as they tried to get the best of Jesus day after day. She came up with all kinds of ideas on how to translate their philosophical questions and debates. She was also the one who solved the dragon problem in Revelation 12 and 13.

None of the supernatural creatures in Machiguenga folklore looked or sounded at all like a dragon. Irene thought about that for a while and then suggested taking advantage of two special syllables that the Machiguengas attached to the names of common jungle animals. For example, if you stuck "niro" onto the end of the word for "monkey," it became a fearsome, powerful, larger than life King Kong reeking of evil. Irene put "niro" on the end of the word for iguana and you could make a monster film out of the result.

While we had friends and family who honored and supported us for the work we did, Irene was more likely to be misunderstood and criticized by her suspicious fellow Machis. Her sacrifices were greater, her measureable rewards much smaller. Still she stuck with it to the end.

Some of the foreign guests attending the dedication ceremonies had been just as faithful, even if in very different ways. Clarence and Verbena Rudd were there for their first visit to Peru. Dad had first met Clarence in the Navy, on the U.S.S. Colorado. Dad was walking around the ship looking for someone to talk to and happened on Clarence, who was sitting in a doorway feeling homesick, lonely and discouraged. Dad and Clarence became fast friends. The Rudds began to support our family around 1950 and have never missed a month in nearly 48 years.

Ernie and Florence Comte had also been friends for life. Dad met Ernie in the Admiralty Islands at the end of World War II. Ernie saw him walking around with a big Scofield Bible under his arm and asked some other sailors who the guy was that carried the Bible. They got acquainted and ended up on the S.S. Medill, a luxury cruiser that had been converted for war.

Even though Dad couldn't and still can't carry a tune, that didn't keep him from organizing a black choir called the Medill Melody Mixers. Ernie was the ship's cook and even though rations were short he somehow came up with little extras for the choir to motivate them to practice.

Charles Miller and his son Doug, part of

my stateside family, were mixed into the crowd. So was the senior pastor of my parents' home church in Indiana, along with several other key partners from the church. Creative detective work would never have been enough without the ongoing prayers and moral support of a vast team of people like these.

Mom and Dad sat in the front row when they weren't busy translating speeches into English or Machiguenga. In a small village just upriver from Huallana, Mom had nearly died of hepatitis. Fortunately a pilot in a float plane got there just in time to save her life. That's why she's still here. Dad's still here because he has a lot of guardian angels.

My parents are the real heroes of my books, though they wouldn't see themselves that way. They are more inclined to shake their heads in amazement at what God did in Machiguenga land, using their strengths and overcoming their weaknesses. They would be the first to say that they weren't perfect, that their decisions weren't always the best and that they learned a lot from the Machis even as they taught them.

Still, it was their faith that took them to Peru, their persistence that kept them there, their trust that allowed us kids to have so many unusual experiences and to grow up as part of the Machiguenga family. It was their steady plodding that finally brought the

Machis their own translation, being handed out now copy by precious copy.

As the dedication service continued, I was asked to make a few remarks. Although my Machiguenga had deteriorated considerably over the years, leaving my grammar sketchy and my vocabulary with big holes in it, I was determined to talk to my friends in their own language. I began with simple greetings, then talked a little about the villages I had been in and some of the people I had known.

In the middle of my talk Dorotea, a retired school teacher, suddenly jumped up from where she had been sitting in the middle of the room. I hadn't seen Dorotea for many years, but she and her sister had been my baby sitters when I was a toddler in Timpia, way back in the beginning. I had first learned the language as they carried me around in handwoven baby slings.

Dorotea worked her way to the edge of the crowd where Mom stood listening and excitedly whispered something into her ear. Later Mom explained what the commotion was about.

"She was so amazed to hear you sound just like a Machiguenga," Mom told me. "She said they need you to come back and be their linguist." For most of the jungle Indians, "linguist" meant someone who would help with education, medicine, development projects and anything else they needed, as Mom and Dad, Harold and Pat Davis, Jerry and Eunice Hamill and so many others had done.

Who can predict life's strange courses? Perhaps some day I will be back. In the meantime, they have the Word and they are using it often. Sometimes I think that they know far more about how to apply it to their lives than I do.

Just a couple of years ago we got word that our friend Pablo had died. According to the Machiguenga kinship system, he was one of Mom's brothers and she sometimes thought of him as a substitute for the brother she had lost when she was adopted away from her birth family as a young child.

Pablo and Dad and Mom had worked closely together on final revisions of the Machi Scriptures. During long tedious days they slogged through the whole New Testament verse by verse. Then in the evenings, when Dad and Mom's brains had completely melted down, Pablo often showed up with a handful of papers to get help on his personal hobby, adapting Spanish hymns into Machiguenga. Mom often groaned inwardly at the prospect of another long evening helping Pablo make his translations more natural and then fit the Machi words to the music. It wasn't easy, but eventually one of Pablo's hymns made it into the Machi hymnbook.

Well, Pablo fell from the rafters of his house one day. His family took him to a clinic downriver, but the nurses couldn't do anything for his serious internal injuries so he was just taken back home.

When Pablo realized he was dying, he told his family, "When I die, don't put any of my things in the grave with me. Father God will have everything I need waiting for me in the house He's getting ready for me." Then he asked them to sing "John," referring to a Machi hymn based on John 14:1-3, where Jesus said, "Now don't be sad. You trust God, trust me as well. There are many houses where my Father lives, and I am going to prepare them for your coming."

When they finished singing, Pablo said, "That's enough now. Sit me up." He folded his hands as though to pray, told them goodbye in typical Machi fashion — "I'm going now" — and went to his Father's house.

When I think of people like Pablo, when I review all of the things God did for us and the Machiguengas, when I remember what Dad and Mom went through to translate the Scriptures, it's no wonder that I cannot hold a copy of the Machiguenga New Testament without getting a lump in my throat. It's there as I write.

Chapter 16

About The Matses

Remember the Matses Indians from the first chapters of this book? In case you're wondering what happened to them....

True to their word, within a couple of weeks after our initial contact several Matses men came back to get Harriet and Hattie. They took them and their belongings to the village, parading them at the front of the line as they entered the village.

The two women found

themselves plunged into a whole new world as they began intensive study of the language and culture. The Matses cared for them in every way and seldom left them alone even when they went to bathe. Most evenings, people came to visit with them and when Harriet asked why, they said, "Because you aren't afraid of the spirits."

Two men from Yarinacocha went to the village to help the Matses men build an airstrip so that Harriet and Hattie could get in and out more easily. The airstrip not only allowed them to bring in medicines and school books, but also provided a way to fly emergency medical cases out. Within a short while people suffering from tiger bites, snake bites and serious falls had all gone to Yarinacocha for help.

The Matses villages were located in such remote areas that it was extremely difficult to help them develop their communities even though they are a very energetic and ambitious people, immediately responsive to suggestions that they feel will improve their lives. Harriet once told me that their intelligence and energy might be due to constant changes in their gene pool as they often stole their wives from other groups than their own.

In any case, community development was as huge a challenge as it was for the Machiguengas. Harriet and Hattie were joined by other SIL colleagues and Peruvian co-workers who focused on that work. The Matses tried a variety of methods to get a reliable meat supply, including fish farming, sheepherding and raising poultry. Along the way some of them became teachers, health workers, dentists and mechanics.

In 1994 I was invited to attend the dedication of the Matses New Testament, 25 years after I had helped contact them. I hadn't kept in close touch with Harriet and Hattie along the way, but there was a strong pull to go back and see what God had done through them. My part had been microscopic compared to theirs, but I still felt like I'd had a part.

That's how I ended up sitting on another hard wooden bench in a church made of palm slats and thatch, along with dozens of Matses Indians and a crowd of white guests from Yarinacocha and the USA.

As the service started, we were suddenly startled to hear the hum of an airplane engine and see everyone around us jump up, cower down and race out of the building to hide behind anything they could find.

"When we first heard airplanes flying toward us," said the laughing chief in the front of the church, "we were so afraid that we hid in the buttress roots of trees. Now we aren't afraid anymore." Apparently someone in the village could mimic an airplane perfectly. The chief concluded his speech by saying that he is very happy. "God is looking well on us. Now that we have the Word, read it and do what it says."

During the years of the translation process, Bible memorization was a key thrust of Harriet and Hattie's work. We listened in awe to a recitation of James 1 in Matses. Part of the awe was that we were listening to a spiritual giant who couldn't walk. Crippled in an accident many years before, Solomon had to crawl from place to place on huge arms and tiny frozen legs. A son had carried him half an hour to attend the dedication. As Harriet's main translation partner through the years, Solomon had memorized most of sixteen books of the New Testament. Spiritually, he had walked farther than I had.

Several different groups were recognized during the dedication service: school teachers, medical workers, pastors, translation helpers and more. Then the first copies were handed out. Harriet graciously called on guests in the crowd to present those copies and even I got the overwhelming privilege of walking slowly up to the front, taking a copy of the Matses New Testament and handing it to a man I still easily recognized. We had first met in the dead of night, in a tiny clearing. When he walked out of the dark jungle, shaking with fear, into the light from flashlights that we held in our hands, little did he or I know that one day I would have the privilege of placing the light of God's Word in his hands.

SPECIAL NOTE

Although these stories may seem unusual to you, they really aren't that different from the experiences of my friends and "family" in SIL.

Members of the Summer Institute of Linguistics and Wycliffe Bible Translators continue to work with minority language groups in every conceivable setting around the world, from towering mountain villages to scorching desert tents to developing cities. The pages of their lives would fill a library and are smeared with sweat, drenched in tears, underlined with laughter and overflowing with love. Their stories could be yours.

There are opportunities for service around the globe using an unbelievable variety of skills and backgrounds. If you would like more information on a most unusual way to give your life, contact Wycliffe Bible Translators USA by calling 1-800-WYCLIFFE or sending e-mail to info.usa@wycliffe.org

P.S. If you decide to join them, start keeping good journals now. Someday, believe me, you'll want to write a book!

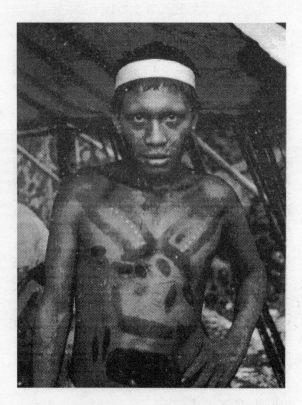

One of the Matses tribesmen who met
Rani on the jungle trail during
the first contact.

Rani Adventure t-shirts are printed with a full color logo and assorted quotes from Rani on white 50/50 blend t-shirts. Shirts are $10 each plus S&h and are available in XL only.

Please send:

_____ Rani t-shirts at $10 ea. _____

Please add $3.00 postage and handling for one shirt plus $1 for each additional shirt.

Shipping & Handling _____

MO residents add sales tax _____

TOTAL ENCLOSED
(Check or money order) _____

Name _____

Address _____

City _____ State ___ Zip _____

MAIL TO HANNIBAL BOOKS, 921 Center Street, Hannibal, MO 63401. Satisfaction guaranteed.

"I'm going now."

Tom Snell

Please send me:

"It's a Jungle Out There!" by Ron Snell. Book One of the Rani Adventures. Ron's life and adventures begin in this fast-paced, hilarious romp through the Amazon jungle.

_____ Copies at $5.95 = _____

"Life is a Jungle!" by Ron Snell. Book Two of the Rani Adventures is full of the exhilarating escapades of Ron's high school years.

_____ Copies at $5.95 = _____

"Jungle Calls" by Ron Snell. Book Three.

_____ Copies at $5.95 = _____

On the 8th Day… God Laughed! by Gene Perret with Terry Perret Martin. 900 jokes arranged alphabetically by topic. Humor that tickles your funnybone while it honors the Creator.

_____ Copies at $5.95 = _____

Way Back in the Kornfields, by James C. Hefley. 900 jokes that will make Grandpa laugh without making Grandma blush.

_____ Copies at $5.95 = _____

Please add $2.00 postage and handling for first book, plus .50 for each additional book.

Shipping & Handling _____
MO residents add sales tax _____
TOTAL ENCLOSED
(Check or money order) _____
Name _____

Address _____

City _____ State ___ Zip _____

MAIL TO HANNIBAL BOOKS, 921 Center Street, Hannibal, MO 63401. Satisfaction guaranteed. Call 1-800-747-0738 for free catalog.